Project Management Institute

GOVERNANCE OF PORTFOLIOS, PROGRAMS, AND PROJECTS: A PRACTICE GUIDE

Library of Congress Cataloging-in-Publication Data

Names: Project Management Institute, publisher.
Title: Governance of portfolios, programs, and projects : a practice guide /
   Project Management Institute.
Description: Newtown Square, PA : Project Management Institute, 2016. |
   Includes bibliographical references.
Identifiers: LCCN 2015040373 | ISBN 9781628250886 (pbk. : alk. paper) | ISBN
   1628250887 (pbk. : alk. paper)
Subjects: LCSH: Portfolio management. | Project management.
Classification: LCC HG4529.5 .G695 2016 | DDC 658.4/04—dc23 LC record available at
http://lccn.loc.gov/2015040373

Published by: Project Management Institute, Inc.
                 18 Campus Blvd., Ste. 150
                 Newtown Square, Pennsylvania 19073-3299 USA
                 Phone: +1 610-356-4600
                 Email: customercare@pmi.org
                 Internet: PMI.org

PMI Publications welcomes corrections and comments on its books. Please feel free to send comments on typographical, formatting, or other errors. Simply make a copy of the relevant page of the book, mark the error, and send it to: Book Editor, PMI Publications, 18 Campus Blvd., Ste. 150, Newtown Square, PA 19073-3299 USA.

To place an order or for pricing information, please contact Independent Publishers Group:

   Independent Publishers Group
   Order Department
   814 North Franklin Street
   Chicago, IL 60610 USA
   Phone: +1 800-888-4741
   Fax: +1 312- 337-5985
   Email: orders@ipgbook.com (For orders only)

10 9 8 7 6 5 4 3 2 1

15 14 13 12 11 POD

TABLE OF CONTENTS

LIST OF TABLES AND FIGURES

PREFACE

Governance of Portfolios, Programs, and Projects: A Practice Guide is a complementary document to PMI's foundational standards. This practice guide provides guidance to organizations and practitioners on how to implement or enhance governance on portfolios, programs, and projects. Although elements of portfolio, program, and project governance appear throughout PMI's foundational standards; this practice guide provides further understanding and differentiation between the types, domains, and functions of governance. Understanding governance as it applies to portfolios, programs, and projects is growing in importance to organizations, because appropriate governance is a factor in the success or failure of strategic initiatives and portfolios, as well as an organization's programs and projects. This practice guide exemplifies PMI's commitment to support the project management profession with a defined body of knowledge.

Governance of Portfolios, Programs, and Projects: A Practice Guide will advance the practice of portfolio, program, and project management while meeting PMI's diverse stakeholder needs. This practice guide is intended to support organizations that are creating an environment to accelerate the implementation of strategy and achievement of organizational objectives while establishing transparency and confidence in decision making and the clarity of roles and responsibilities. This practice guide will advance the topic of portfolio, program, and project governance by capturing those practices from conceptualization to implementation that practitioners and organizations find informative and useful. Governance is a broad and complex topic, with many dimensions, levels, relationships, and types that may exist within or across an organization. It's important to recognize that organizations may adopt principles, practices, processes, and policies that are translated into actions regarding governance at the organizational, portfolio, program, and project levels. As execution of governance at each of these levels may vary, this practice guide focuses on the common actions and outcomes that may be undertaken by portfolio, program, and project practitioners to effectively and efficiently assess, plan, implement, and improve governance for OPM and individual portfolio, program, and project management levels. This practice guide describes a common governance framework aligning OPM and portfolio, program, and project management and provides four governance domains of alignment, risk, performance, and communications. The four governance domains enable the core governance functions of oversight, control, integration, and decision making, which are integral processes to achieve effective portfolios, programs, and projects.

A practice guide is a new category in the PMI library of standards, which is intended to encourage discussion related to areas of practice where there may not yet be consensus. Innovation, combined with a dynamic external environment, drives the need for organizations and practitioners to act more decisively and become more adaptive to ensure that the appropriate level of governance exists. PMI introduced this practice guide to identify useful approaches for integration with PMI's foundational standards.

Practice guides are developed by leading experts in the field using new processes that provide reliable information and reduce the time required for development and distribution. PMI defines a practice guide as a standards product that provides supporting supplemental information and instructions for the application of PMI standards. Practice guides are limited consensus-based standards products and do not go through the exposure draft process. However, the resulting work may be introduced later as a potential standard, and if so, will then be subjected to PMI's documented process for the development of full consensus standards.

1

INTRODUCTION

1.1 The Purpose and Need for this Guide

This practice guide provides guidance to practitioners and organizations for the governance of portfolios, programs, and projects. This practice guide strives to advance the topic of portfolio, program, and project governance by capturing practices from conceptualization to implementation, which practitioners and organizations should find informative and useful. This guide presents the following:

- Reference for portfolio, program, and project governance for senior executives, functional managers, as well as senior portfolio, program, and project management leadership;

- Definition, implementation, and management of effective portfolio, program, project, and organizational project management (OPM) governance;

- Practices for creating a governance framework; and

- Guidance for most organizations, including governmental, nongovernmental for-profit, and not-for-profit private and public entities that may be implementing or enhancing governance for portfolios, programs, and projects.

Implementation of an effective portfolio, program, and project governance framework within an organization can be challenging due to factors such as increasing business complexities, regulatory requirements, globalization, and rapid changes in technology and business environments. Other challenges may include inadequate governance, executive sponsorship, support, and understanding of portfolio, program, and project management. For projects and programs executed by more than one organization (e.g., a joint venture), governance becomes more complex. Any governance framework should be dynamic and responsive in adapting to changing portfolio, program, and project environments. Effective governance of portfolios, programs, and projects focuses not only on compliance with policies, procedures, laws, and regulations, but also on informed judgment regarding decision making to meet organizational objectives.

People at every level of the organization and external stakeholders have an impact on the governance framework for portfolios, programs, and projects. This topic is of great interest to organizations, because ineffective governance is often noted in literature and research findings as a source of project delays, failures, or other negative consequences. Moreover, there is minimal holistic treatment of this topic in portfolio, program, and project management literature. In 2014, the Project Management Institute (PMI) did an extensive review of extant research published in the fields of project management and allied disciplines regarding governance of projects, programs, and portfolios. For an overview of those findings, see Appendix X2. An effective governance framework can help to ensure an organization's alignment of strategy and its subsequent execution by providing appropriate oversight, leadership, and guidance.

This practice guide uses the term "organization" to refer to an entire or subset of a company, agency, association, or business unit, including for-profit, not-for-profit, and government organizations.

1.2 The Intended Audience

This practice guide is intended for practitioners and organizations that would like to create an environment to accelerate the implementation of strategy and achievement of organizational objectives while establishing transparency and confidence in decision making and clarity of roles and responsibilities. This practice guide applies to all types and sizes of organizations and may include:

- Board of directors or their representatives;
- Executives;
- Nonfunctional management staff that may be responsible for oversight of portfolios, programs, and projects;
- Members of portfolio, program, and project management offices (PMOs) and centers of excellence;
- Portfolio, program, and project management practitioners;
- Portfolio, program, and project team members and stakeholders;
- Functional managers, including those who manage portfolio, program, and project management professionals; and
- Educators, consultants, and process specialists in portfolio, program, and project management.

1.3 Overview of the Practice Guide

This practice guide is organized in a structured fashion so the user is able to locate section(s) that are of particular interest. It is not necessarily written to be read in its entirety, but rather to allow users to focus on the specific section(s) that are of greatest interest. Some information is repeated in one or more sections so that each individual section may be understood on its own and at the individual portfolio, program, and project governance level. It is recommended that the user begin by reading Section 1 (Introduction) prior to reading any other sections of interest as follows:

- **Section 2: Organizational Project Management (OPM) Governance.** Describes OPM governance; tailoring governance; governance relationships and considerations; roles and responsibilities; and domains, functions, and processes. Describes how governance can be implemented as a governance program or project for integrated portfolio, program, and project governance.
- **Section 3: Governance at the Portfolio Level.** Describes portfolio governance; governance relationships and considerations; roles and responsibilities; and domains, functions, and processes. Describes how governance can be implemented within a portfolio management process cycle.
- **Section 4: Governance at the Program Level.** Describes program governance; governance relationships and considerations; roles and responsibilities; and domains, functions, and processes. Describes how governance can be implemented within a program life cycle.

- **Section 5: Governance at the Project Level.** Describes project governance; governance relationships and considerations; roles and responsibilities; and domains, functions, and processes. Describes how governance can be implemented within a project life cycle.

1.4 Overview of Governance Related to Portfolio, Program, and Project Management

Governance is an enabler of good portfolio, program, and project management and also an important element for successful portfolios, programs, and projects. Governance typically focuses on who makes the decisions (decision rights and authority structures), how the decisions are made (processes/procedures), and collaboration enablers (trust, flexibility, and behavioral controls), thereby defining the governance framework within which decisions are made and decision makers are held accountable.

When discussing governance, it is important to distinguish that there are various types that may exist:

- **Governance of organizations.** Many organizations have principles, policies, and procedures to provide guidance for how an organization is directed and controlled. Organizational governance principles are approved by the organization's highest-level governing body and may include clarity of roles and authorities, ethics, accountability, transparency, social responsibility, and a variety of other principles that are unique to each organization. Organizational policies are the mechanism used to support and communicate these principles so that the governing board or body is informed of the key strategic issues and risks facing an organization.

- **Governance of portfolio, program, and project management.** Some organizations institute organization-wide policies and procedures to oversee and direct portfolio, program, and project practices across multiple portfolios, programs, and projects. Governance at this level may direct how areas of organizational governance are directly linked to individual portfolio, program, and project activities, and are focused on how the portfolio, program, and project management capability is governed overall.

- **Governance of portfolios, programs, and projects.** This practice guide is focused on how governance is defined and carried out to ensure the success of portfolios, programs, and projects, which includes describing the details of processes, activities, and tasks needed in order to successfully implement or enhance governance of the portfolio, program, or project to produce the desired outcomes or results.

There is no consistent approach to portfolio, program, and project governance in the various organizations and contexts in which they exist. There are multiple definitions of governance in the literature and standards; confusion exists in distinguishing among the governance needs at different levels of portfolio, program, and project management. There are different levels of governance inherent in portfolio, program, and project management, including organizational governance; organizational project management (OPM) governance; and portfolio, program, and project governance. To help bring needed clarity, this practice guide provides definitions for governance in order to distinguish their differences as well as indicate their common elements. Definitions used in this practice guide are unique to the governance of portfolios, programs, and projects. The definitions of governance are:

- **Organizational governance.** A structured way to provide control, direction, and coordination through people, policies, and processes to meet organizational strategic and operational goals. Organizational governance is typically conducted by a board of directors to ensure accountability, fairness, and transparency to its stakeholders. It typically includes legal, regulatory, compliance, cultural, ethical, environmental, risk, social responsibility, and community functions. Organizational governance principles, decisions, and processes have an impact on the governance of portfolios, programs, and projects. For example, in the United States, the Sarbanes-Oxley Act of 2002 requires management to certify the accuracy of organizational financial reporting. This has a direct impact on the rigor and frequency of reviews for portfolio, program, and project financial controls and reporting.

- **OPM governance.** The framework, functions, and processes that guide organizational project management activities in order *to align portfolio, program, and project management practices* to meet organizational strategic and operational goals.

- **Portfolio governance.** The framework, functions, and processes that guide portfolio management activities in order *to optimize investments* to meet organizational strategic and operational goals.

- **Program governance.** The framework, functions, and processes that guide program management activities in order *to deliver business value* to meet organizational strategic and operational goals.

- **Project governance.** The framework, functions, and processes that guide project management activities in order *to create a unique product, service, or result* to meet organizational strategic and operational goals.

Governance terms commonly used in this practice guide are unique to governance of portfolios, programs, and projects and are defined as follows:

- **Governing body.** A temporary or permanent organized group consisting of members by areas of responsibility and authority to provide guidance and decision making for portfolios, programs, and projects (e.g., boards, steering committees).

- **Governance framework.** The four governance domains with functions, processes, and activities for portfolios, programs, and projects. Domains and functions are described in Sections 1.6 and 1.7 and in Sections 2 through 5.

- **Governance domain.** A grouping of functions carried out by an individual, group, or organization to address a specific governance area of concentration. Described in Section 1.6.

- **Governance function.** A grouping of processes related to each other and across governance domains that are performed in order to support governance for portfolios, programs, and projects. Described in Section 1.7.

Figure 1-1 represents the basic elements of governance that are found in most organizations that execute business strategies through portfolios, programs, and projects. The elements have both a connected and a

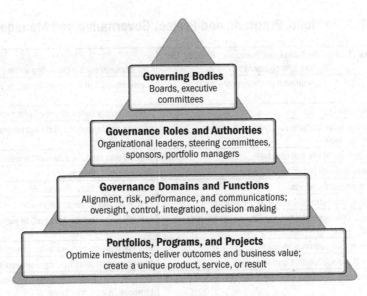

Figure 1-1. Governance Elements

hierarchical-type relationship. Figure 1-1 presents the dimensions of governance in a simplified manner; in reality, governance is recognized as a complex concept. Governance-related elements are dynamic and should adapt to the changing organizational, portfolio, program, and project environments. The relationship between the complexity of programs and projects and governance resources is discussed in Section 1.5.2.

1.5 Portfolio, Program, and Project Governance versus Portfolio, Program, and Project Management

Portfolio, program, and project governance focuses on overseeing and approving the framework, functions, and processes to provide guidance and decision making for portfolios, programs, and projects.

Portfolio, program, and project management are the implementation activities that are defined, planned, and executed to achieve organizational strategic and operational goals through individual portfolios, programs, and projects.

Portfolio, program, and project governance activities are those that provide guidance, decision making, and management oversight, whereas the portfolio, program, and project management activities are specific to organizing and doing the work of portfolios, programs, and projects. Within an organization or specific portfolio, program, or project, governance and management activities may overlap because there are functions and roles that may be assumed by the same person or group of people. In some organizations or in a particular portfolio, program, or project, governance and management roles may be combined. On some portfolios and programs, the portfolio or program manager may assume a governance role. Table 1-1 shows an example of the key differences between governance and management activities. Although these activities are shown in two columns, one for governance

Table 1-1. Portfolio, Program, and Project Governance and Management Activities

Governance (What)—Decisions and Guidance; Oversee and Ensure Management	Management (How)—Organizing and Doing the Work
Define and approve organizational strategy, goals, and objectives	Recommend and implement strategy, goals, and objectives
Make and determine policy	Communicate policy and establish procedures
Establish and approve portfolio, program, and project governance framework	Identify and document portfolio, program, and project governance framework
Ensure engagement of key stakeholders	Identify and manage stakeholder relationships
Determine and approve prioritization criteria	Prioritize components
Authorize components and mix	Select and optimize components
Identify, ensure, and communicate strategic alignment	Communicate strategic alignment
Determine and communicate risk appetite and thresholds; resolve risks/issues	Identify and escalate risks and/or issues
Request, review, and authorize changes	Identify, request, and authorize changes
Determine and provide funding and resources	Identify and request funding and resources
Approve, terminate, or cancel portfolio, program, and/or project	Recommend portfolio, program, and/or project approval, termination, or cancellation
Determine and approve roles, responsibilities, and decision-making authorities	Recommend and communicate roles, responsibilities, and decision-making authorities
Approve charters, plans, and/or business cases	Create charters, plans, and/or business cases
Determine and/or approve key performance indicators (KPIs)/measures	Monitor/measure KPIs; create/consolidate reports
Review and approve integrated roadmap	Create or update integrated roadmap
Review, approve, and/or authorize phase gates and/or reviews	Manage phase gates and/or reviews
Authorize audits	Conduct audits
Review and approve organizational change management	Define and implement organizational change management plans
Accountable for portfolio, program, and project results	Responsible for portfolio, program, and project results
Review and approve portfolio, program, and project methodology	Communicate and adhere to portfolio, program, and project methodology

and one for management, the activities in either column may be adapted based on the organizational context. The number of activities in either column does not mean that the activities are equal or that the amount of work effort is comparable.

Figure 1-2 demonstrates the portfolio, program, and project governance relationship with organizational governance and shows the portfolio, program, and project management relationship with organizational management. Governance activities ensure that management activities are defined, planned, and implemented within portfolio, program, and project management. Management activities are more operational and tactical than governance activities, which are more strategic and focus on oversight and guidance. Portfolio management may contain more governance activities and fewer management activities relative to program or project management, as portfolio management is a governance mechanism of organizational-level governance used to ensure strategic alignment with organizational objectives. Governance provides oversight and direction for management to ensure the right work is done and also that the work is done right through organizational project management. Please refer to Section 2.2 for more information on organizational project management.

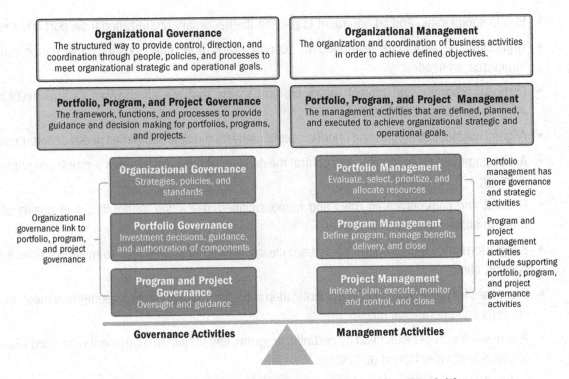

Figure 1-2. Governance Activities vs. Management Activities

1.5.1 Effective Governance of Portfolios, Programs, and Projects

Achieving effective governance can be very challenging in most organizational environments. Any governance framework should be dynamic and adaptive to the organization's needs, resources, and culture in order to be effective. One approach to achieve effective governance is through continuous improvement, which is a strategy where organizations develop the ability to achieve higher standards and adjust to changing conditions by incrementally implementing improvements in ongoing cycles. Continuous improvement requires a structured organizational change management strategy and plan, including implementing rewards systems, engaging stakeholders, and adapting communications to each stakeholder group to ensure that changes are effective and sustained. Just as successful organizations do not evolve randomly, implementing effective governance is a large-scale change initiative that should have a purposeful and adaptive strategy that can anticipate, influence, and respond effectively to organizational needs. Most important, there is not a one-size-fits-all approach to governance. Governance needs to fit the organizational structure, culture, and complexity in order to be effective. The following are characteristics of effective governance and management oversight:

- Defined and integrated governance framework and approach that is aligned with existing organizational structures and organizational strategy and objectives;
- Competent and capable governing bodies that provide timely guidance and oversight;
- Leadership that is adaptable, flexible, and responsive to the changing needs of the organization, portfolio, program, project, and team;

- Visible sponsorship and commitment to provide the necessary organizational support and resources;

- Organizational structures leveraged to support PMOs and other existing governance organizational structures, as needed;

- Portfolio, program, and project managers and teams that are empowered to effectively deliver and remove barriers and obstacles;

- Aligned business strategies and priorities, particularly for multiple competing needs or resource contention;

- Active engagement to monitor and control the delivery of business benefits through program and project delivery;

- Defined and communicated roles and responsibilities, delegated authorities, and quality standards in order to allow accelerated decisions;

- Key performance indicators (KPIs) that are clearly defined and measured to minimize risks and enhance opportunities;

- Processes for proper selection and prioritization of program and project components to meet organizational strategy and operational goals;

- Processes for proper execution by portfolio, program, and project management combined with adherence to policies, standards, and guidelines;

- Tailored communication, knowledge management, training, and reporting;

- Structured organizational change management approach for continuous improvement;

- Engaged stakeholders to develop processes and support change; and

- Adequate funding to develop, maintain, and improve governance.

1.5.2 Governance and Program and Project Complexity

There is a relationship between the required governance resources and processes and the complexity of programs and projects, *Navigating Complexity: A Practice Guide* [1][1] defines complexity as a "characteristic of a program or project or its environment which is difficult to manage due to human behavior, system behavior, or ambiguity." As program and project complexity increases, typically the required governance authority structure, resources, and processes increase as well. Other factors that could impact the governance required are risk appetite, culture, and project management maturity.

In order to balance risk and efficiency, it is important to consider program and project complexity as the governance authority structure, resources, and processes are applied. When there is a lower level of rigor in governance processes or authority structures than required, risk is introduced; on the other hand, when there is an excess level of rigor in governance, inefficiency results, because resources and processes consume valuable

---

[1] The numbers in brackets refer to the list of references at the end of this practice guide.

time and effort. When implementing governance, keep in mind that it should involve the least amount of authority structure, resources, and processes as possible, because time and costs are associated with governance decision-making and oversight activities. Governance processes should be tailored to the program and project complexity, risks, and other factors. By adopting a flexible and responsive approach to tailoring governance processes, an organization can achieve the optimal level of efficiency. The governance and program and project complexity relationship is depicted in Figure 1-3.

- **Scenario A.** This scenario indicates that the governance resources and processes are greater than required based on program and project complexity, resulting in inefficient governance. This is due to governance that uses more resources and processes than required, which consumes valuable resources. Governance needs to be tailored to the complexity of the program and project to eliminate bureaucracy but also achieve the proper level of oversight and leadership.

- **Scenario B.** This scenario indicates that the existing governance resources and processes are less than required based on the program and project complexity resulting in risks to program and project execution and the achievement of strategic goals and objectives. In other words, as the complexity of

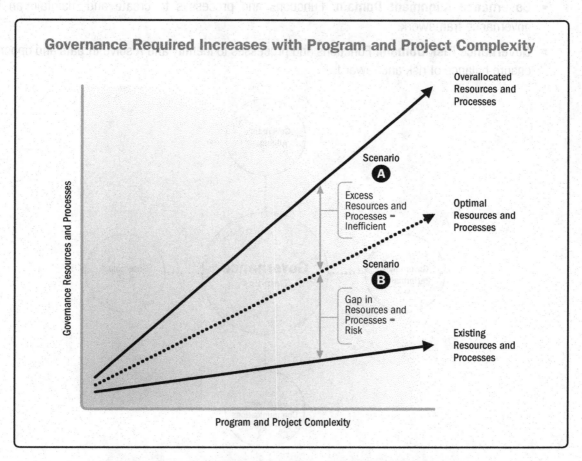

Figure 1-3. Governance and Program and Project Complexity

programs and projects increases, the governance resources and processes should also increase. The gap between existing and optimal resources and processes results in risk. An example of the gap is where an executive sponsor may be spread across multiple programs or projects, thus presenting risk and ineffective governance.

1.6 Governance Domains

This practice guide presents the governance framework by grouping closely related functions into the four domains that uniquely represent governance: governance alignment, governance risk, governance communications, and governance performance (see Figure 1-4). Governance domains are complementary groupings of related functions that uniquely characterize and differentiate the processes or activities found in one governance domain from another. A portfolio, program, or project manager may actively carry out work within multiple governance domains during the portfolio, program, and project life cycles.

These four governance domains are further detailed in Sections 2 through 5, and are described as follows:

- **Governance Alignment Domain.** Functions and processes to create and maintain an integrated governance framework.

- **Governance Risk Domain.** Functions and processes to identify and resolve threats and opportunities to ensure balance of risk and reward.

Figure 1-4. Governance Domains

- **Governance Performance Domain.** Functions and processes to ensure measurement and evaluation of KPIs against parameters and realization of business value.
- **Governance Communications Domain.** Functions and processes to disseminate information, engage stakeholders, and ensure organizational change.

1.7 Governance Functions

Within each of the four governance domains, there are governance functions that categorize critical processes, activities, and tasks that are performed to provide for an organization's portfolios, programs, and projects.

The four governance functions shown in Figure 1-5 are oversight, control, integration, and decision making, which represent a continuing sequence of processes, activities, and tasks that can occur in any direction and may be repeated throughout the portfolio, program, or project life cycle:

These four governance functions are further detailed in Sections 2 through 5, and are defined as follows:

- **Oversight function.** The processes and activities that provide guidance, direction, and leadership for portfolios, programs, and projects.
- **Control function.** The processes and activities that provide monitoring, measuring, and reporting for portfolios, programs, and projects.
- **Integration function.** The processes and activities that provide strategic alignment for portfolios, programs, and projects.
- **Decision-making function.** The processes and activities that provide structure and delegations of authority for portfolios, programs, and projects.

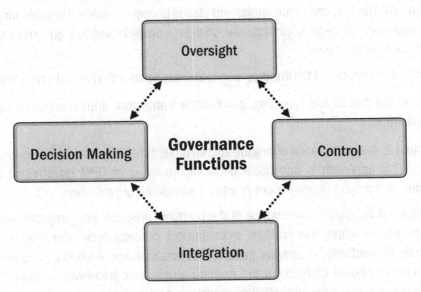

Figure 1-5. Governance Functions

1.8 Governance Framework Implementation

In order to improve an existing or implement a new governance framework to support an organization's portfolios, programs, or projects, this guide describes a four-step method that should be followed: *Assess, Plan, Implement,* and *Improve.* These steps may be overlapping and iterative, and may be performed multiple times throughout the framework implementation. The implementation should be tailored to the culture of the organization; the types of portfolios, programs, and projects managed; and the needs of the organization to meet strategic objectives. All of the activities and deliverables described in this practice guide may not apply to all organizations, and there may be other activities and deliverables required based on the organizational context. Each organization should consider the specific governance framework that would be the most appropriate to implement and tailor it accordingly. Additional tailoring considerations are described in Section 2.3.1.

Figure 1-6 represents the high-level governance framework implementation four-step method that is further detailed in Sections 2 through 5 and in Annex A1.

The four steps to implement a governance framework are:

- **Assess.** The purpose of the assess step is to review and analyze the current state of governance in the organizational context and current versus desired portfolio, program, and project governance practices. Performing assessments and analysis will assist the organization; portfolio, program, and project managers; and sponsors in developing a consistent vision and method for the future state of governance for portfolios, programs, and projects.

- **Plan.** The purpose of the plan step is to plan for the desired future state governance in order to establish the governance organizational structure, roles, responsibilities, and authorities; governance-related processes; and required interactions.

- **Implement.** The purpose of the implement step is to operationalize the governance framework, functions, and processes; manage organizational change; complete various governance reviews; and measure governance performance.

- **Improve.** The purpose of the improve step is to assess performance and define improvement opportunities.

This practice guide details the four-step governance framework implementation, focusing on two different scenarios or applications.

- In Section 2, the governance of organizational project management (OPM) is implemented as a separate project. This approach is applicable because the focus of OPM governance is to integrate portfolio, program, and project management practices across the organization.

- In Sections 3 through 5, governance at the portfolio, program, and project levels utilizes the framework implementation within the portfolio management process cycle, the program life cycle, and project life cycle, respectively, to provide guidance to practitioners. Portfolio, program, and project managers and sponsors should understand the existing governance framework and ensure that the appropriate framework is in place for all portfolios, programs, and projects.

Annex A1 describes in detail the portfolio, program, and project governance framework implementation steps.

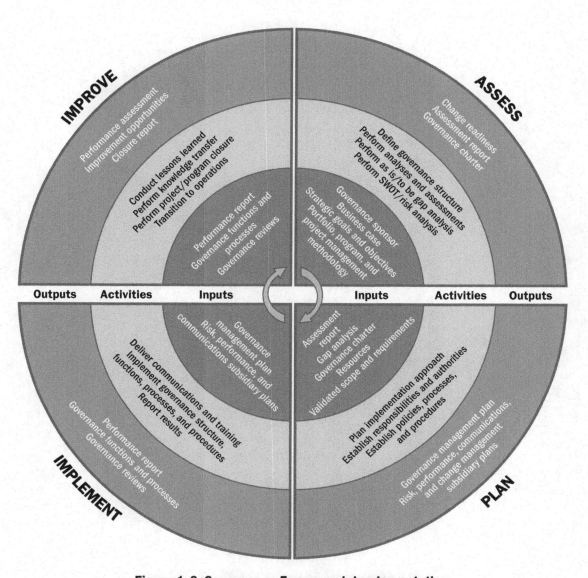

Figure 1-6. Governance Framework Implementation

2

2

ORGANIZATIONAL PROJECT MANAGEMENT (OPM) GOVERNANCE

2.1 Overview

Over the past few decades, there has been an increasing focus on portfolio, program, and project success in order for organizations to realize their strategic goals. Furthermore, there is an increasing need to manage portfolios, programs, and projects in an integrated manner in order to realize benefits; attain efficiencies; improve productivity; optimize the use of scarce resources; achieve compliance; improve customer satisfaction; achieve successful portfolio, program, and project completion; or achieve faster speed to market that would not be possible if managed on an individual basis.

This section provides the framework, processes, and implementation approach to help organizations establish or improve governance that oversees organizational project management (OPM). It is recommended that the reader begin by reading Section 1 (Introduction) and then any other sections of interest.

2.2 OPM

Organizational project management (OPM) provides a strategy execution framework to align portfolio, program, and project management practices with organizational strategy and objectives, customized as needed according to the organization's context, situation, or structure. This section of the practice guide leverages and builds upon OPM practices and guidelines as detailed in *Implementing Organizational Project Management: A Practice Guide* [2] as well as *Organizational Project Management Maturity Model (OPM3®): Knowledge Foundation* – Third Edition [3].

OPM governance provides guidance, decision making, and oversight for the OPM strategic execution framework. There is an emphasis on OPM as a strategic execution framework for organizations to manage through integration and alignment of portfolio, program, and project management practices. OPM governance focuses on oversight and decision making of the strategic execution framework in order to maximize the organization's value. Figure 2-1 illustrates the dimensions of governance and management across the OPM and portfolio, program, and project levels.

2.3 OPM Governance

OPM governance is defined as the framework, functions, and processes that guide organizational project management activities in order to align portfolio, program, and project management practices to meet organizational strategic and operational goals. OPM governance includes the policies, procedures, and systems through which organizational leadership directs, defines, authorizes, and supports the alignment of strategy and organizational goals.

	Governance (What) — Decisions and Guidance; Oversee and Ensure		Management (How) — Organizing and Doing the Work
Organizational Project Management Level	OPM governance is the framework, functions, and processes that guide organizational project management activities in order to align portfolio, program, and project management practices to meet organizational strategic and operational goals.		OPM is a strategy execution framework that utilizes portfolio, program, and project management as well as organizational-enabling practices to consistently and predictably deliver organizational strategy to produce better performance, better results, and a sustainable competitive advantage.
Portfolio Level	Portfolio governance is the framework, functions, and processes that guide portfolio management activities in order to optimize investments and meet organizational strategic and operational goals.		Portfolio management is the centralized management of one or more portfolios to achieve strategic objectives.
Program Level	Program governance is the framework, functions, and processes that guide program management activities in order to deliver business value and meet organizational strategic and operational goals.		Program management is the application of knowledge, skills, tools, and techniques to a program to meet the program requirements and to obtain benefits and control not available by managing projects individually.
Project Level	Project governance is the framework, functions, and processes that guide project management activities in order to create a unique product, service, or result and meet organizational strategic and operational goals.		Project management is the application of knowledge, skills, tools, and techniques to project activities to meet the project requirements.

Figure 2-1. Governance and Management Definitions at Organizational, Portfolio, Program, and Project Levels

OPM governance is one of four core-enabling processes for OPM implementation; the other core-enabling processes are strategic alignment, competency management, and organizational project management methodology. When implementing OPM governance, it is important to also consider how the other core-enabling processes are integrated into the OPM management plan overall:

- Strategic alignment ensures portfolios, programs, and projects support achievement of business objectives;

- Competency management ensures that skills are developed and available when needed to implement portfolios, programs, and projects; and

- Organizational project management methodology provides the structure (people and processes) necessary to implement portfolios, programs, and projects.

OPM governance is not a stand-alone process, but one that overlaps with, has an impact on, and is impacted by related organizational and portfolio management processes, including organizational strategy and goals, resource management, risk management, and performance management. OPM governance is an organization-wide approach to achieving project management excellence in all areas, and should be integrated with governance at all levels.

Figure 2-2 depicts the interactions of OPM governance-related activities with portfolio, program, and project management activities. These interactions are also detailed in Sections 3 through 5.

2

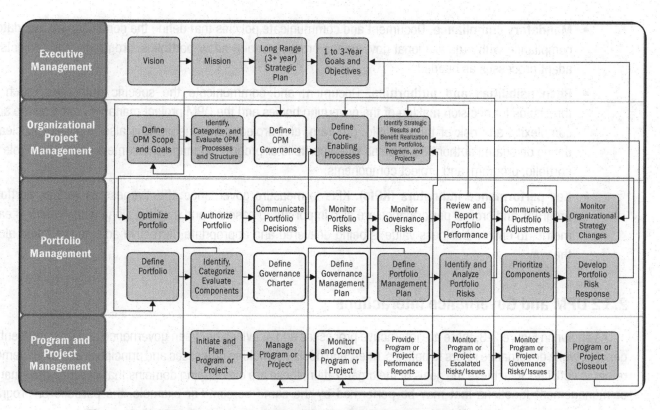

Figure 2-2. OPM Governance Interactions with Portfolios, Programs, and Projects

2.3.1 Tailoring the Approach to OPM Governance

The purpose of tailoring an approach to governance is to consider the politics, culture, external stakeholders, and the environmental and regulatory factors in organizations. Based on these influences and factors, varying levels of governance may be required.

Another key consideration is whether OPM governance is being implemented for the first time or is being enhanced. Formal governance may not exist within the organization or it may exist only at the individual portfolio, program, or project level. The approach to implementing governance should be tailored based on these factors and the governance fit with the organization's needs.

The OPM governance framework implementation steps are an iterative process to implement generally recognized good practices and are adaptable and flexible according to the desired outcomes to support governance implementation. For more information regarding the framework implementation steps, see Section 2.6.

Organizations may tailor their approach to OPM governance based on the following:

- **Size, complexity, and risks.** Determine the level of governance according to portfolio, program, or project types based on size (resources, organizational span), complexity, level of risk, priority, and the resulting decision making required. Considerations such as organizational risk tolerance; understanding of existing governance structures; and portfolio, program, and project practices are also important.

- **Mandatory compliance.** Document and communicate policies that define the conditions for mandatory compliance with organizational governance processes, and allow portfolios, programs, and projects to adapt processes as needed.

- **Responsibilities and authorities.** Document and communicate the specific authorities, such as thresholds for decision making of the governing bodies and the OPM project manager based on the size, complexity, and risk of the portfolio, program, and project components. It is also important to clearly define delegated authorities, such as when portfolio or program managers assume a governance role for portfolio, program, and project components.

- **Key performance indicators (KPIs).** KPIs to measure governance effectiveness as well as portfolio, program, and project performance are also important to baseline and monitor, along with owners of each metric, to ensure business value is being delivered and appropriate corrective actions are taken along the way.

2.3.2 OPM and Governance Interactions

As shown in Figure 2-3, there are interactive processes and activities between governance and management. In general, while governance refers to policies, rules, and decision-making processes and principles, and management refers to activities to achieve the goals of the organization, these are overlapping domains that describe governance or management functions that may be performed by the same person. For example, the portfolio or program

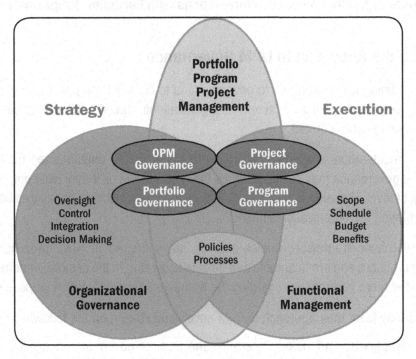

Figure 2-3. Governance and Management Interactions and Relationships

manager may perform a governing role on a portfolio or program, but the portfolio or program manager is also responsible for the portfolio and program management processes. Portfolio, program, and project management leverages policies and processes from both domains.

Governance processes guide strategic oversight, control, decision making, and integration, whereas management processes guide the tactical execution of scope, schedule, budget, and benefits realization. Since OPM and portfolio governance processes are strategic, these areas set the policies and procedures for portfolio, program, and project management, whereas individual project or program governance oversees the tactical execution. Governance at the individual portfolio, program, or project level is focused within their specific sphere of influence, whereas OPM governance guides integrated portfolios, programs, or projects to implement organizational governance standards, policies, and processes.

It is also important to note that governance and management may exist at levels that differentiate specific functions, as well as offer specific considerations:

- **Organizational governance.** Oversee the entire organization, focusing on setting the strategic direction, legal, fiduciary, and oversight functions along with boundaries. There should be strategy and organizational policies and processes that will need to be cascaded to portfolios, programs, and projects.

- **OPM and portfolio management.** Setup of the appropriate governance framework is needed to integrate the organizational strategy into portfolios, programs, and projects.

- **Program and project management.** Setup of the appropriate governance framework is needed to oversee the management execution.

- **Functional management.** Resources, constraints, and current practices may need to be considered; some functional managers may become members of governing bodies for portfolios, programs, and projects.

There may be a hierarchy of governance levels that is simplified in a smaller organization, but is more complex in a matrixed, global organization. Organizational and OPM governance frameworks, decision-making authorities, and boundaries or limits should be clearly defined and communicated as well as the policies and processes to which portfolios, programs, and projects are required to adhere.

2.3.3 OPM Governance Considerations

OPM governance may take on any number of forms or organizational structures based on the overall organizational needs, culture, business structure, context, and environment, which could include characteristics such as multinational; department; governmental agency; nongovernmental organization (NGO); internal or external customers; developing economy or market; tangible or intangible product, service, or result; budget; new product development; or operations.

Another OPM governance consideration is the integrated governance processes. Integrated governance processes are a critical component of the governance activities and include strategic alignment; prioritization criteria; and authorization of portfolio, program, and project components and allocation of internal resources to accomplish organizational strategy and objectives. Governance levels are linked together to ensure that each organizational action is ultimately aligned with the defined organizational strategy. As with any large-scale change initiative, culture and organizational change management need to be integrated with the overall OPM governance implementation plans.

Table 2-1 identifies types of organizations and the governance structure that aligns best with the organization. In addition, cultural influences should be considered, including organizational vision, mission, values, regional differences, regulatory policies, and risk tolerances; view of leadership, hierarchy and authority; and motivation and reward systems.

Table 2-1. Influence of Organizational Structure on Governance

Governance Framework	Functional/Regional	Functional/Enterprise	Integrated Organizational Structure
Governance Scope	Single function, region, or department only	Functional across multiple regions (i.e., IT across all sites)	Entire organization or function
Governance Authority	Portfolio-, program-, or project-specific	Integrated across multiple portfolios, programs, or projects	Integrated across the entire organization's portfolios, programs, and projects and portfolio, program, and project management practices
Governance Role	Part-time functional or administrative coordinator	Part-time mixed (may be functional or portfolio/program/project manager)	Full-time OPM project manager assigned
Governance Process Maturity	Only to meet specific functional or project needs	Processes in place for quarterly or annual review across PPP	OPM governance processes continuously improved

As shown in Figure 2-4, there are various governance structures that may be implemented in an organization, which reflect the organization's existing structures and processes. While some are more top-down approaches with various hierarchies, other governance structures may be flatter in nature but with functions spread across multiple areas, or may be specific to an individual portfolio, program, or project.

2.4 Roles and Responsibilities

This example responsibility assignment matrix (RAM) is a RACI (responsible, accountable, consult, and inform) chart shown in Table 2-2. The grid shows the governance roles assigned and the governance domain action/decision areas. It is used to illustrate the connections between governance action/decision areas and governance roles. RAMs may be developed for multiple, integrated governance levels and by individual portfolio, program, and project governance levels. This is a high-level example for OPM-integrated governance for portfolios, programs, and projects.

RAMs at the individual portfolio, program, and project governance levels may be used within the individual governance teams to designate roles, responsibilities, and decision-making authorities for specific actions, decisions, and activities. The matrix format shows all the actions/decisions associated with one person or role and all people or roles associated with one action/decision. The sample chart shows the actions/decisions by governance domain in the left column. The assigned resources or roles can be shown as individuals or groups. A RACI chart is a useful communications tool to ensure clear divisions of roles, expectations, and decision-making authorities.

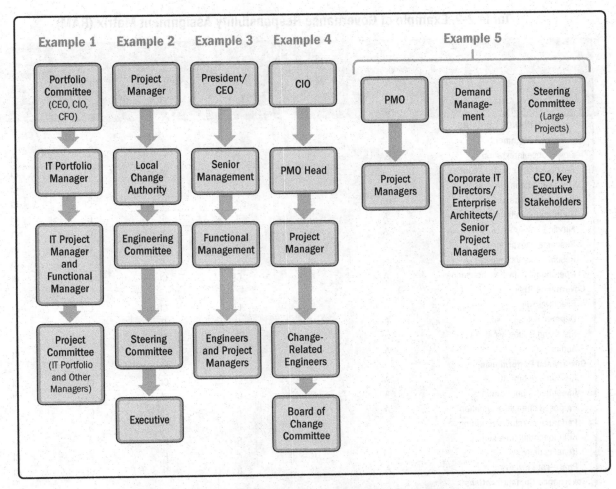

Figure 2-4. Examples of Various Governance Structures

2.4.1 OPM Governing Body

The governing body is the temporary or permanent organization (sometimes called a group, committee, or board) that is accountable for the overall success of OPM governance, and integration with other governing bodies (organizational or function) as well as alignment of portfolio, program, and project practices. The sponsor, senior management, OPM project manager, or portfolio or program manager may be part of the governing body.

2.4.2 OPM Sponsor

A sponsor is a person or group that provides resources and leadership for OPM governance, and is accountable for enabling success. An active, engaged, and visible sponsor is crucial and should be designated with the proper organizational authority, resources, and influence in order to remove barriers and provide the day-to-day guidance to ensure the success of OPM governance since it has an organization-wide scope that may cross functional and organizational boundaries.

Table 2-2. Example of Governance Responsibility Assignment Matrix (RAM)

Actions/Decisions	OPM and Governance of Portfolios (Portfolios inclusive of programs and projects)	Portfolio Managers	Program Managers	Project Managers	Portfolio Sponsors	Other Portfolio Stakeholders
GOVERNANCE DOMAINS						
Governance Alignment						
Governance integration	RA	CI	CI	CI	CI	CI
Responsibilities and authorities	A	R	CI	CI	CI	CI
Decision criteria/process	A	R	CI	CI	CI	CI
Governance budget	RA	CI	I	I	CI	CI
Prioritization criteria	A	R	I	I	CI	CI
Funding investments	A	R	I	I	CI	CI
Resource allocation	A	R	I	I	CI	CI
Resource commitments	A	CI	I	I	R	CI
Operational activities integration	A	R	CI	CI	CI	CI
Governance Risk						
Risk thresholds	A	R	CI	CI	CI	CI
Dependencies tracking	A	R	R	R	I	I
Risks and issues escalation	A	R	R	R	CI	CI
Audits	A	R	R	R	CI	CI
Governance Performance						
Resource optimization	A	R	CI	CI	CI	CI
Investment optimization	A	R	CI	CI	CI	CI
Proposed changes evaluation	A	R	R	R	CI	CI
Performance/status reporting	CI	R	R	R	A	CI
KPI monitoring/measuring	I	R	R	R	A	CI
Benefits delivery	CI	R	R	R	A	CI
Phase-gate reviews	A	R	R	R	CI	CI
Governance Communications						
Stakeholder engagement	CI	RA	R	R	CI	CI
Integrated roadmap	A	R	CI	CI	CI	CI
Communications coordination	I	R	R	R	CI	CI
Communicate decisions	A	R	CI	CI	CI	CI
Organizational change management	CI	R	R	R	A	CI
Messages to organization	A	R	CI	CI	CI	I

R = Responsible for completion   A = Accountable for decision   C = Consult before action or decision   I = Inform after action or decision

2.4.3 OPM Project or Program Manager

In order to effectively implement or enhance OPM governance, a dedicated project or program manager should be assigned to manage an OPM governance framework implementation project or program. (For simplicity, this section will use OPM project manager, although it is acknowledged that it may be a program manager, depending on the organization.) The OPM project manager is responsible for the effective planning, execution, monitoring, and delivery of the project according to the OPM governance charter.

2.4.4 Portfolio, Program, and Project Manager

The portfolio, program, and project managers are responsible for ensuring that the overall portfolio, program, and project governance framework aligns with the OPM governance framework and objectives as detailed in the OPM governance management plan and for clearly communicating the framework and processes to all stakeholders.

2.4.5 PMO (Portfolio, Program, or Project Management Office)

PMO refers to a portfolio, program, or project management office and supports portfolio, program, and project functions, respectively. The PMO in an organization may be the entity that defines and maintains the process standards related to portfolio, program, or project management. The PMO may be the implementer or recipient of OPM governance, since there may be many types of PMOs within an organization that differ in scope, authority, reporting hierarchy, and responsibilities.

Depending on organizational needs, culture, and structure, the PMO may operate on an enterprise, business unit, divisional, or functional level (e.g., IT, R&D, and marketing). There may also be specific-purpose PMOs based on the need of the organization. For example, an enterprise resource planning (ERP) PMO may be formed to manage the implementation of ERP, which can affect every person in the organization due to the human resource and financial process implications. The establishment of a PMO may highlight the need for a structured and formalized governance framework where none existed, and the PMO may assume governance functions.

A PMO may support or lead OPM governance in the following ways:

- Developing organizational governance frameworks, hierarchies, and relationships;
- Overseeing portfolio, program, and project strategic alignment and facilitating key decisions;
- Overseeing the integration of portfolio, program, and project processes;
- Aligning and optimizing portfolio, program, and project components; supporting component proposals and evaluations; facilitating prioritization and authorization; and allocating resources;
- Developing and maintaining portfolio, program, and project management standards and methodologies;
- Negotiating and coordinating resources between portfolio, program, and project components or between portfolios;
- Assessing and escalating issues and risks;
- Conducting detailed reviews for portfolios, programs, and projects;
- Monitoring portfolio, program, and project performance (actual versus planned) and key performance indicators;
- Conducting legal, regulatory, environmental, financial, and compliance audits;
- Monitoring compliance to policies and procedures;

- Facilitating organization-wide stakeholder engagement and agreement; and
- Assigning portfolio, program, and project managers to implement components.

2.5 OPM Governance Domains, Functions, and Processes

The OPM governance framework groups key processes into four domains that are related areas of activity or functions that uniquely characterize and differentiate the activities. The four OPM governance domains are: OPM governance alignment, OPM governance risk, OPM governance performance, and OPM governance communications. Within each domain, there are four main functions:

- **Oversight.** Provide overall guidance and direction to PPP.
- **Control.** Establish appropriate controls, audits, and reviews, including reporting and risk management activities.
- **Integration.** Integrate strategy with execution of portfolios, programs, and projects.
- **Decision making.** Establish decision-making processes across portfolios, programs, and projects.

Table 2-3 reflects the mapping of the four OPM functions into the four OPM governance domains. Each of the key OPM processes is shown in the domain in which most of the process takes place; however, activities may be iterative and span across areas. These are not role specific and pertain to all activities in the governance domains.

Table 2-3. OPM Governance Related Processes by Domains and Functions

Functions Domains	Oversight	Control	Integration	Decision Making
OPM Governance Alignment Domain	• Perform organizational strategic alignment • Establish governing body • Create OPM governance charter • Conduct periodic planning for prioritization and funding	• Create OPM governance management plan	• Align portfolio, program, and project execution with organizational strategy • Integrate portfolio, program, and project processes • Create integrated portfolio, program, and project roadmap	• Establish OPM decision-making process • Determine portfolio, program, and project component prioritization and funding
OPM Governance Risk Domain	• Manage portfolio, program, and/or project internal or external dependencies	• Create OPM risk management plan • Establish OPM risk escalation process	• Integrate dependency management	• Resolve and remediate escalated risks and/or issues
OPM Governance Performance Domain	• Conduct portfolio, program, and project reviews and audits	• Create OPM performance management plan • Establish OPM reporting and control processes • Monitor KPIs	• Perform integrated performance reporting • Align resource capacity and capability needs across portfolios, programs, and projects	• Optimize portfolio, program, and project resources • Assess changes to organizational strategy or portfolio, program, and project performance
OPM Governance Communications Domain	• Communicate key messages to organization	• Create communications management plan • Monitor communication effectiveness	• Disseminate communications	• Report decisions made with justification

2.5.1 OPM Governance Alignment Domain

The OPM governance alignment domain includes defining the OPM governance charter and OPM governance management plan; establishing the governing body; integrating the hierarchy of portfolio, program, and project governance; monitoring the adherence to governance management plan; and establishing a decision-making process.

- **OPM governance charter.** The OPM governance charter authorizes the formation of the governing body and authorizes the governing body to apply resources to implement governance-related activities.

- **OPM governance management plan.** The OPM governance management plan describes how the governance framework, functions, and processes will be performed including governance roles, responsibilities, and decision-making structures.

- **OPM governing body.** The OPM governing body should be established to ensure continuous alignment with organizational strategy and the delivery of OPM results, as well as optimized governance framework. The OPM governing body is responsible for oversight of portfolio, program, and project management. Portfolio, program, and project managers are responsible for adherence to the OPM governance framework, including integration with their existing portfolio, program, and project governance. Since there may be multiple hierarchies and types (functional or organization-wide) of governance in an organization, a governing body should establish a decision-making framework and determine who will make what kind of decisions and in what scenarios as detailed in the governance management plan. Based on the decision-making framework, the governing body should determine whether portfolio, program, and project components should be changed or terminated.

2.5.2 OPM Governance Risk Domain

The OPM governance risk domain includes the following activities or tasks:

- **Risk management plan.** Create a risk management plan. The OPM governance risk management plan presents how the OPM project manager will manage risks through the implementation of governance.

- **Risk tolerances.** Identify risk tolerances and thresholds, and establish a risk escalation process. Establish integrated escalation processes for risks and issues and include in the risk management plan, with thresholds for resolution at various levels.

- **Dependency management.** Integrate dependency management across portfolios, programs, and projects.

- **Audits.** Conduct portfolio, program, and project audits. Monitor portfolio, program, and project performance and audit based on risk and complexity.

- **Internal/external dependency review.** Review internal/external dependencies of portfolios, programs, and projects. Monitor internal and external dependencies between portfolios, programs, and projects as well as the risks and other external elements. Internal and external dependencies should be reviewed by the OPM governing body.

- **Escalated risks and issues.** Approve recommendations to resolve escalated risks and issues. In order to resolve and remediate risks and/or issues, the OPM project manager should escalate them to the governing body for decisions, as there may be broader impacts across the organization. Include the risks and/or issues in the OPM dashboard reporting and reviews, following risk and issue escalation processes.

2.5.3 OPM Governance Performance Domain

The OPM governance performance domain includes the following activities or tasks:

- **Integrated performance management plans.** Create integrated performance management plans. The OPM governance performance management plan may be included as a part of an OPM governance management plan or it may be a separate plan. The plan should include expected performance to ensure that OPM delivers the expected result, both qualitatively and quantitatively. Reporting structure and control processes can be established as part of this plan.

- **Integrated reporting and control processes.** Review integrated reporting and control processes. It is also important to provide performance reporting to the governing body, sponsor, PMO, and key stakeholders. This is one of the key domains that enable the OPM project manager to collect the necessary data for performance measurement.

- **Reviews.** Review portfolio, program, and project component results. The governing body should monitor the performance of components as outlined in the performance management plan through performance reviews, such as audits, gate reviews, and portfolio reviews. Performance data should be evaluated to ensure KPIs are within expected parameters and resources are optimized.

- **KPIs.** Review KPIs. Some organizations employ KPIs to measure performance for scope, schedule, budget, benefits, and quality.

- **Proposed changes.** Approve proposed portfolio, program, and project changes. Proposed changes to the portfolio, program, and project components that may impact results should be evaluated and determined by the governing body.

2.5.4 OPM Governance Communications Domain

The OPM governance communications domain includes the following activities or tasks:

- **Communications management plan.** Create a communications management plan. The OPM governance communications management plan may be a part of the OPM governance management plan or may be a separate plan. The plan should describe how and when elements such as project-level risks, performance, and project results should be reported to the governing body, sponsor, and key stakeholders. The plan should also describe how and when various governance decisions are communicated and include how to get feedback from key stakeholders.

- **Communications.** Disseminate communications. The OPM governing body should provide transparency through communication and decisions to portfolio, program, and project managers; sponsors; the

PMO; and key stakeholders. The OPM governing body should monitor communication based on the communication plan and take actions to improve communication.

- **Justification for decisions.** Report decisions made and provide justification for those decisions. Decision making by governance should be transparent, documented with justification, and reported to stakeholders. Roles, responsibilities, and decision-making authority should be communicated.

2.6 OPM Governance Framework Implementation

In order to implement or enhance OPM governance, a project or program should be initiated using four implementation steps through continuous improvement cycles:

- **Assess.** Assess current state of governance; develop vision for future state of governance; perform gap analysis.

- **Plan.** Develop detailed governance management plan to implement or improve governance as a project.

- **Implement.** Implement the plan, including organizational change management.

- **Improve.** Identify improvements, conduct performance measurement, and plan for the next iteration.

Figure 2-5 represents a typical iterative process optimization and improvement project cycle. It shows the continuous effort that an organization needs to exercise in order to maintain high performance in its governance framework. It is important to note even when the implementation of a governance framework requires a continuous

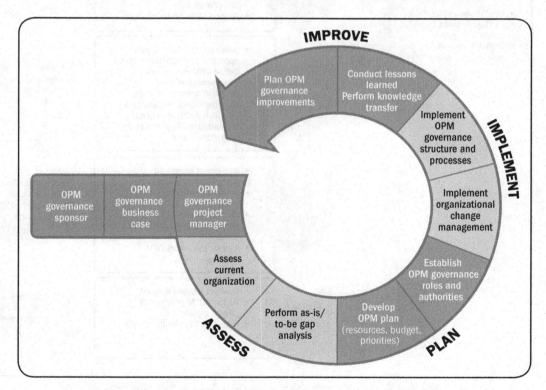

Figure 2-5. OPM Governance Framework Process Improvement Cycle

process, it should be led at the organization level with the structure and authority over the integrated portfolios, programs, and projects. These steps may be accomplished in an overlapping or in a linear progression. Successive iterations of the framework demonstrate continuous improvement, which is a generally recognized good practice.

To be effective, the implementation of an OPM governance framework should be performed as a specific program or project. The size and the complexity of the organization are factors to take into account when choosing the best methodology between the program or project implementation approach. Once the program or project is initiated, assessment of the organizational needs can begin.

Since OPM and portfolio management focus on the setup of the appropriate governance framework to integrate the organizational strategy into portfolios, programs, and projects, it is highly recommended that the activities and deliverables in Section 3 be reviewed and considered in addition to Sections 4 and 5 for program and project governance framework implementations and detailed descriptions of the four-step activities and deliverables.

A summary of an OPM governance implementation framework is shown in Figure 2-6; the details are described in Sections 2.6.1 through 2.6.5.

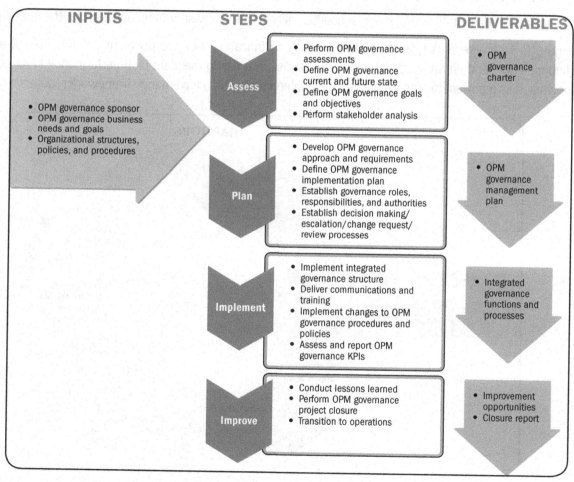

Figure 2-6. OPM Governance Framework Implementation

2.6.1 Assess

Assessing the needs for OPM governance involves identification of the authorizing organization's requirements, expectations, and specific organizational inputs and outputs, which are then integrated into an assessment of the organization's change readiness for OPM governance.

This first step is important in order to understand the current state of OPM governance, the authorizing organization's expectations, vision for the future state, and the processes that are to be implemented. Performing an assessment in various areas of the organization against a future state view identifies gaps, which will assist with the development of an effective OPM governance framework and overall program. Several techniques may be used to gather information such as surveys and open-ended questions during interviews or work sessions.

The inputs of the assess step include:

- Strategic goals and objectives;
- Prior organizational governance assessments;
- Organizational structures, policies, and procedures;
- Understanding of existing management teams or governing bodies and current governance structures;
- OPM governance sponsor;
- Portfolio, program, and project management methodologies;
- Governance business need and/or value (business case);
- Portfolio, program, and project capability and capacity assessments; and
- Portfolio, program, and project inventory, status, and performance.

To execute the assess step, some key activities are:

- **Perform analyses and assessments.** Include change readiness assessment, culture, and organizational structure. Determine what may impact the success of governance implementation. Perform stakeholder analysis and identify and engage key stakeholders to understand the culture, politics, and concerns. Areas to assess include portfolio, program, and project management capabilities and capacity; PMOs; information systems; knowledge management; audit support; education; and training in order to determine the current accountabilities and decision authorities for governance oversight and the effectiveness of the current system and methods.

- **Define OPM governance deliverables.** These deliverables may include integrated governance structure including decision-making authorities, support structure, communications, training, functions, processes, and procedures.

- **Define OPM governance framework.** This is the governing body's decision-making framework. The framework should include roles, responsibilities, and authorities. The OPM governance structure may be separate from the organizational structure or may be integrated. It is important to define the relationships and accountabilities to other governing bodies and structures in the organization.

- **Perform SWOT/risk analyses.** Analyze the strengths, weaknesses, opportunities, and threats and determine the impacts of risks identified to the attainment of OPM governance goals and business objectives.

- **Validate OPM governance scope, requirements, and critical success factors.** It is critical to engage key stakeholders to determine scope, requirements, and critical success factors. Identify what is in and out of scope in addition to organization areas that are impacted.

Considerations during the assessment step are as follows:

- Every organization has its own internal governance framework that affects the effort required during the assess step. There are considerations such as the existence of portfolio, program, and project governance; organization size; existing portfolio, program, or project methodologies; number of and structure of existing governing bodies that may help to establish a more accurate estimation of the cost; and resources needed to implement the OPM governance framework.

- Organizations that do not have an existing governance framework will likely struggle to achieve consistent and sustainable governance.

- Organizations that have already implemented portfolio, program, and/or project governance frameworks are better prepared to extend them to the entire organization, which reduces costs and the required amount of resources for the OPM governance implementation.

The key deliverables of the assess step are:

- Assessment report and current and future state gap analysis, and

- OPM project governance charter.

The other outputs from the assess step are:

- Need for OPM governance is clarified;

- Organization's change readiness is defined and understood; and

- Scope of the governance implementation and change is approved.

The assessment included in the gap analysis and assessment report should describe the current state, gaps, and the desired future state as follows:

- Current portfolio, program, and project management policies and practices;

- Current OPM and other governance models (when applicable);

- Existing governance capabilities and structure including PMOs;

- Degree of OPM governance model integration within the organization;

- Current governance model membership and decision-making authorities;

- Enterprise environmental factors and organizational process assets (policies and procedures, portfolio management information system, and lessons learned);

- Organizational change management needed for an effective governance implementation;

- Gap analysis based on vision of future state of OPM governance;

- Organization's change readiness evaluation;
- Scope of the governance implementation; and
- Acceptance by the organization's management to undertake the proposed transformation.

Table 2-4 shows an example of assessing the current state of portfolio, program, and project governance in an organization prior to implementation of OPM governance with three potential scenarios:

- **Scenario 1.** Illustrates that when portfolio, program, project governance frameworks do not exist, or exist only at the individual portfolio, program, or project level, it is not recommended to begin with an OPM governance implementation, because effort, cost, resources, and organizational change management may be prohibitive. The overall recommendation is to start with a portfolio governance framework to begin the alignment of individual program and project governance.

- **Scenario 2.** Illustrates that when there are existing and aligned program and project frameworks, as well as some individual portfolio frameworks, it may be possible to begin implementing an OPM governance framework.

Table 2-4. Example OPM Governance Assessment Tool

		Scenario 1	Scenario 2	Scenario 3
OPM Governance Recommendation		No common governance framework; significant effort and resources required. Recommend to start at individual portfolio or program levels prior to OPM governance implementation.	Good framework exists at program and project levels. May begin OPM governance implementation, although resources, time, and organizational change management will need to be a focus.	Framework exists in all areas; recommend OPM governance implementation. Focus on alignment and integration of existing frameworks.
OPM Governance Assessment		Effort, cost, resource, and alignment needs are high. Organizational change management will also be a challenge.	Effort, costs, and organizational change will need planning and consideration. May have opportunity to leverage existing governance frameworks at project or program levels and attain efficiencies.	Effort and costs may not be a factor due to the potential to leverage existing frameworks or structures. Portfolio governance can be extended at the organizational level. Organization embraces governance as an effective way of achieving goals.
Portfolio, Program, and Project Framework	**Portfolio Governance**	No portfolio governance framework exists. Decision making is inefficient and ineffective. Processes may be redundant with multiple areas of individual governance structures.	Some individual portfolio governance framework exists, but there is no alignment between portfolios, programs, and projects.	Overall portfolio governance exists with common framework and alignment with programs and projects. Processes are controlled and continuously improved.
	Program Governance	Governance framework may exist but mostly specific for each program. Governance bodies are not aligned between portfolios, programs, and projects.	Program governance exists with common framework, including integration with projects. Results are measured against intended benefits.	Program governance is monitored and controlled to achieve intended benefits with projects. Programs share common governance framework and good practices and are continuously improved.
	Project Governance	Some individual project governance framework may exist. Governing bodies are not aligned. Processes may be redundant or not shared, and no continuous processes are in place.	Overall governance framework exists and may be aligned between projects. Results can be measured. Governing bodies understand the benefits and are engaged.	Governance framework exists and it is monitored and controlled. Governing bodies are engaged and aligned. All projects use the same governance framework and are continuously improved.

The overall recommendation is to focus on leveraging, aligning, and enhancing the PPP frameworks, and consider effort, cost, and organizational change management that will be required to implement.

- **Scenario 3.** Illustrates that when portfolio, program, and project governance frameworks exist and are aligned, it is recommended to begin the OPM governance framework implementation, focusing on integrating and streamlining governance across the existing structures. The main focus may be leveraging existing structures' processes and reducing potential overlapping authorities and responsibilities, thereby attaining efficiencies as enabling timely decision making.

As the key output of the assess step, the OPM governance charter provides the OPM project manager with the authority to apply resources to implement or enhance OPM governance functions and processes. Chartering governance describes the linkage to existing organizational governance and describes how governance will deliver value to the organization.

The OPM governance charter should include:

- **Goals and objectives.** State the goals and objectives of implementing OPM governance; identify and set up the governing bodies; identify new governance functions or processes to be improved; and determine critical success factors, KPIs, and results expected.

- **Alignment of governance across organizations.** Specify how OPM governance will be integrated across the existing organizational structures, including the processes for setup or change of governance organizational structure; establish or change responsibilities, authorities, and thresholds.

- **Problem statement and business benefits.** Identify the business need and the value to be delivered; link the need and value to the strategy, mission, vision, and goals of the organization. Identify influencers such as complexity, politics, culture, structure, and internal/external stakeholders.

- **In and out of scope areas for governance.** Clearly describe the scope of governance, including a description of the impacted single, multiple, or specific functions of the organization; identify which policies and related functions to improve and which new processes to implement.

- **Timeline and budget.** Determine milestones, resources, and budget required to implement or enhance governance.

- **Key assumptions, constraints, dependencies, and risks.** Consider resource, budget, and operation limitations.

- **Team members and roles.** Identify the OPM governance sponsor, functional leads, PMO, and other key members, as applicable.

The OPM governance charter provides key inputs to the plan step.

2.6.2 Plan

The second step is planning for the implementation of the future state of the new or enhanced OPM governance framework, functions, and processes. The outcomes of this step are a governance management plan that defines the approach and how it will be implemented and managed. When planning for change, people and cultural issues should be taken into consideration. Therefore, the organization should engage stakeholders when planning the approach, transition, and integration of governance changes. Based on the organization's extent of governance changes, the governance management plan should balance organizational culture, structure, and change readiness with the implementation approach. An approach that ensures early, incremental progress should be considered, especially for organizations with a history of resistance to change.

The plan step activities are:

- **Plan integrated governance approach and requirements.** Determine the integrated approach for the implementation of functions and processes, how they will be integrated into existing governance frameworks, success factors, and key stakeholder requirements. Develop an integrated roadmap of changes over time in prioritized phases, depending upon the level of change, and the timing to design, develop, and test processes. The planning should consider how to leverage existing resources or processes, as it may be possible to streamline existing governance frameworks, and attain efficiencies.

- **Develop project schedule.** The schedule may include the key sequence for activities, resources required, and effort.

- **Establish governance roles, responsibilities, and authorities.** Identify the governing body members, roles, responsibilities, and decision-making authorities. This may include the roles, responsibilities, and decision-making authorities of the PMOs, portfolio, program, and project managers, and sponsor(s). Although the OPM governance framework may expand some responsibilities, it may also reduce other responsibilities on individual portfolios, programs, and projects. The OPM governance organizational structure, along with the relationship and hierarchies to other governing bodies, should be established.

- **Establish governance functions and processes.** Define the identified functions and processes to be created or enhanced, as well as thresholds for oversight and decision making. Some portfolio-, program-, and project-specific areas include:

  o Prioritization and funding;

  o Decision-making hierarchies, including what types and thresholds are delegated to portfolios, programs, and projects;

  o Risk appetite, attitude, and escalation;

  o Reviews and audits;

  o KPIs; and

  o Integrated reporting.

- **OPM governance framework implementation planning.** The example shown in Figure 2-7 lists key questions that can be used to develop an OPM governance management plan. The questions provide a starting point and are grouped into the following areas:

  o Assess the current state of OPM governance.

  o Assess the future state of OPM governance.

  o Plan how to communicate OPM governance to the organization.

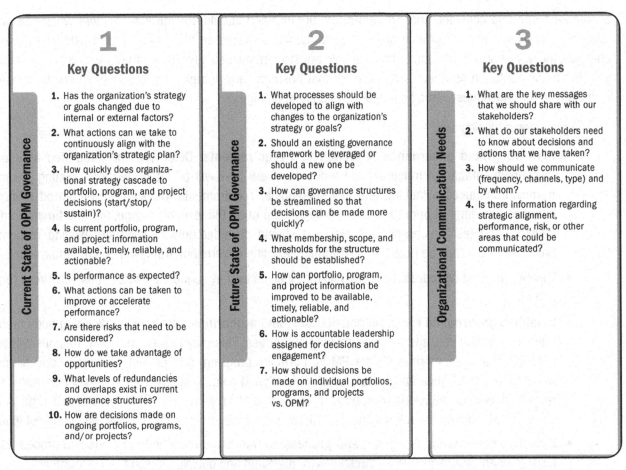

Figure 2-7. OPM Governance Framework Implementation Planning

The OPM governance management plan is the key output of the plan step, and should include:

- **Introduction and background.** Provide a general background on the previous assess step, including the business need.

- **Goals and objectives.** Align plan with the charter's objectives and scope.

- **Risks, dependencies, assumptions, and constraints.** List key risks, dependencies, assumptions, and constraints including organizational, resource, budget, and operational limitations.

- **Timeline and budget.** Include the anticipated milestones, phases, and financial investment requested to implement OPM governance.

- **OPM governance structure.** Include a description of the new or changed governance structure (body, boards, and steering committees), members, roles, responsibilities, and decision-making authorities.

- **Team members, roles, and responsibilities.** Identify team members, roles, and responsibilities for the team that will manage the implementation of the new or changed governance processes.

2

- **Stakeholder matrix.** List the stakeholders or groups to be engaged and communicated with, based on roles, interests, or expectations during the design, implementation, and support of the governance processes.

- **Governance functions and processes.** Describe the approach to the design, implementation, and improvement of governance functions and processes in the plan. Describe how the functions and processes will be integrated and transitioned to business as usual. A generally recognized good practice is continuous improvement; therefore, the plan may provide for periodic reassessments to measure progress and detect adjustments required.

- **KPI metrics and measurement.** Identify the KPI methods and measurement techniques that will be used to evaluate the OPM governance adoption. These KPI methods and measurement techniques should be baselined and periodically collected, consolidated, and reported. There may be KPIs around the effectiveness and efficiency of OPM governance (e.g., cost and time of decision making); adoption; and collective portfolio, program, and project performance (e.g., success rate of portfolios, programs, and projects before and after implementation).The KPIs can be reported on a balanced scorecard or dashboard to reinforce the value proposition of OPM governance.

- **Organizational change management.** The plan to enable organizational change should be described and should include engaging key stakeholders to champion the change, benefits, and impacts. Various methods and channels should be leveraged, along with opportunities to provide two-way dialogues and incorporate feedback.

- **Communications and training.** This should describe the communications and training during the design, implementation, and support of the governance processes.

- **Supporting functions.** The areas where support is needed should be identified, such as existing PMOs and other areas (i.e., finance, IT, etc.) that may be leveraged. The feedback and support approach during and after implementation of processes should be described.

The completed OPM governance management plan should be approved by key stakeholders and communicated broadly to the organization, especially senior management, and those who are required to be involved for a successful implementation. The governance management plan is the key input to the implement step.

2.6.3 Implement

During the implementation step of OPM governance, the implementation team designs the policies, procedures, and processes for OPM governance and then executes the governance management plan to roll out OPM governance across the organization.

This step involves the development of details to implement the future state for an OPM governance framework. The OPM governance implementation teams may conduct surveys, workshops, and interviews in order to develop the input into the OPM project deliverables. The team implements OPM governance in accordance with the OPM governance management plan, such as developing or enhancing the functions and processes, establishing or modifying the governing body's responsibilities and scope of authority, preparing the organization for change, and operationalizing the changes.

The implement step activities are:

- **Implement integrated governance structure.** Establish the new or changed governance structure (body, boards, and steering committees), members, roles, responsibilities, and decision-making authorities. This may include meeting calendar coordination and related communications.

- **Implement organizational change management.** Provide organizational change management support during and immediately after implementation based on the needs previously identified. Include details on the means to request and receive support from the team members or stakeholders. Conduct periodic surveys to gauge the acceptance of change and implement any corrective actions needed.

- **Deliver communications and training.** Prior to the implementation, communicate and train stakeholders based on needs. Communicate the events and timeline. Report and track attendance, feedback, and results for potential required changes. Determine the change readiness to proceed with the implementation.

- **Implement new or enhanced governance functions, processes, and procedures.** Design and document the functions and processes. This may include policies, procedures, tools, and techniques. A formal policy may indicate which processes and tools are required by the organization. Based on the complexity and risk of change, pilot the processes and make required updates prior to a broader implementation. Conduct feedback sessions after the pilot. When enhancing processes or tools, a pilot may not be necessary.

- **Assess and report OPM results.** Upon implementation, begin to collect, consolidate, and report on the predefined metrics and measurements, such as performance of the processes, level of adoption of the changes, and results based on the performance parameters identified in the implementation plan. Adjust the plan to address any discrepancies.

The key deliverables of the implementation activities are:

- KPI measurements for both OPM governance effectiveness/efficiency, as well as portfolio, program, and project performance;
- Operationalized functions and processes; and
- Integrated governance reviews.

Other outputs of the implementation activities may include (note that some of these elements may exist and require updating):

- OPM governance templates,
- Policies, and
- Procedures.

Some documents that are used by the governing body may also be part of the deliverables from the implementation step. Examples of these documents are:

- Procedures explaining how and when governance at the organizational level is to be performed (i.e., meetings, purpose, scope, etc.);

- Policies (those predefined decisions for specific situations);
- Process to manage changes in the governing body, scope, authorities, and membership;
- Procedures explaining how and when the governance framework is updated and how change requests are to be addressed; and
- Templates for each committee from all levels (organizational, portfolio, program, and project).

Figure 2-8 shows another example of how decision-making committees are organized. This model can also be used as a common structure for every committee when decisions are part of the expected results. The benefit of this kind of model is that it allows governing bodies to be aligned with every decision-making committee (at any level) and to see who will be responsible to bring information, perform analyses, and make decisions.

At the close of the implement step, implementation activities are complete and the new or enhanced OPM governance framework, functions, and processes have been operationalized. The deliverables of the implement step are inputs to the improve step.

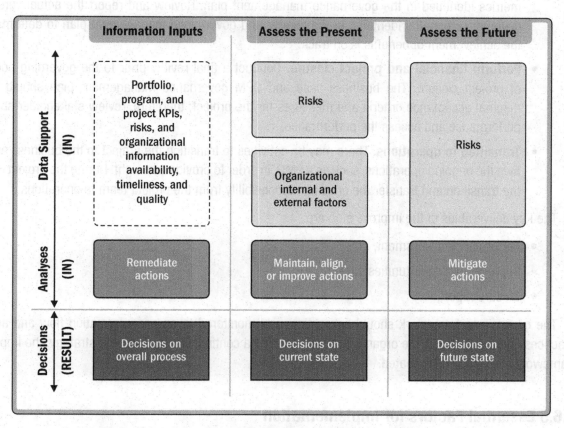

Figure 2-8. Canvas for Governance Meetings (Based on Decision Making, Communication, Performance, and Risk Factors)

2.6.4 Improve

The improve step is the fourth and final step to evaluate the implementation from the previous step (Section 2.6.3). The improve step includes conducting lessons learned, assessing performance, identifying potential future changes, transitioning to operations, and project closure. The outcomes of this step may be the beginning of an integrated continuous process improvement. There may be situations where OPM governance needs to expand or gaps may be found that require improvement by identifying these conditions and then prioritizing and executing an improvement initiative.

The improve step activities are:

- **Conduct lessons learned.** Conduct lessons learned and gather feedback on the implementation from stakeholders. Document, share, and add the feedback and lessons learned information to the organization's knowledge base for future improvements. Prior to the next implementation, review lessons learned and feedback for good practices.

- **Assess performance and benefits realized.** After monitoring and reviewing the new or enhanced processes, evaluate, measure, and report the adoption and results based on the KPI methods and metrics identified in the governance management plan. Review and report the actual versus planned governance benefits identified in the charter and governance management plan to determine whether the achievement of benefits is on track.

- **Perform financial and project closure.** Conduct a final review prior to the governing body approval of project closure. The business case and OPM governance management plan should specify the minimal acceptance criteria and measures for the project; therefore, review stakeholder satisfaction of performance and assess the performance.

- **Transition to operations.** There may be activities to transition the project to the business area that will own the ongoing operations, such as a PMO, in order to provide oversight. During the project closure, plan the transition and transfer the ongoing responsibility from the project team to operations.

The key deliverables of the improve step are:

- Performance assessment,
- Improvement opportunities, and
- Closure report.

The governance framework should be continuously monitored to ensure information flow and adherence to practices and processes. If the organization has adopted a continuous improvement strategy, the implementation framework steps may be repeated.

2.6.5 Essential Factors for Implementation

There are several factors essential for implementation of OPM governance, including the support of and expectations of executive and senior management; the engagement of other organizational departments or groups;

types and numbers of portfolios, programs, and projects; and other organizational frameworks and governance structures. These factors can be simple or complex, based on the diversity and intricacy of the organization's structure and size.

- **Senior management support.** Visible and active management commitment and sustained leadership are required for successful governance implementation and enhancements. Full support and buy-in at the executive level greatly improve the chances for a successful governance implementation.

- **OPM governance authority.** An overall OPM governing body (boards, committees) with decision-making authorities should be established with defined relationships and hierarchies to other governing bodies and organizational structures. The governing body should define the types and levels of changes that require governance review and approval versus those that may be delegated to the portfolio, program, or project level.

- **Governance functions and processes.** It is critical that the governance functions, processes, and responsibilities are documented and communicated.

  - The OPM governing body should have primary responsibility for assuring quality standards and compliance with mandatory practices and processes, such as reporting and control processes related to status, scope, milestones, risks, benefits, changes, and financial performance.

  - There should be sustained, committed leadership for reviewing integrated portfolio, program, and project results against the organization's strategic plan and objectives and making decisions related to funding, resource allocation, risk or issue escalation, and requested changes.

  - Stakeholders should be engaged continuously, especially before, during, and after changes to the OPM governance framework, functions, and processes, in order to achieve effective governance.

3

GOVERNANCE AT THE PORTFOLIO LEVEL

3.1 Overview

This section describes portfolio and portfolio management, portfolio governance, roles and responsibilities, domains, functions and processes, and a proposed approach for implementing a governance framework within a portfolio management process cycle. This section also includes portfolio governance relationships and considerations. It is recommended to begin by reading Section 1 (Introduction) first and then any other sections of interest.

Portfolio governance is essential and critical to help enforce accountability, optimize investments, and escalate issues to the appropriate decision makers. Portfolio governance also provides the ability to align strategic decisions across business areas and improve communication.

Portfolio-governing bodies make decisions about strategic alignment, investments, and priorities for the portfolio, which include programs, projects, and operations, and guides how these decisions are made.

3.2 Portfolio and Portfolio Management

The Standard for Portfolio Management – Third Edition [4] defines a portfolio as "projects, programs, subportfolios, and operations managed as a group to achieve strategic objectives." A portfolio or portfolios exist to achieve one or more organizational strategies and operational goals. Portfolios have a scope that changes with the strategic objectives of the organization. The success of a portfolio is measured by the optimization of investments and the performance of the portfolio.

Portfolio management, as defined in *The Standard for Portfolio Management* – Third Edition, is the centralized management of one or more portfolios to achieve strategic objectives. Portfolio management provides a mechanism for governance, enables portfolio governance functions to support the decision-making activities of a governing body, and ensures investment optimization.

3.3 Portfolio Governance

Consistent with organizational governance, portfolio governance is established to provide guidance and oversight of the portfolio management function in order to optimize investments and meet organizational strategic and operational goals. The key difference between portfolio governance and program or project governance is that portfolio governance focuses on providing guidance to achieve the portfolio targets that are aligned with the organizational strategies and operational goals while ensuring investment optimization is achieved. It provides guidance on how to best use the limited resources and assets and integrates operational activities with the program and project work to meet the portfolio targets. In addition to this practice guide, *The Standard for Portfolio Management* – Third Edition provides additional information on portfolio management processes.

3.3.1 What is Portfolio Governance?

This practice guide defines portfolio governance as "the framework, functions, and processes that guide portfolio management activities in order to optimize investments and meet organizational strategic and operational goals." The term "governance framework" refers to the four governance domains with functions, processes, and activities for portfolios, programs, and projects. Governance functions are a grouping of processes related to each other and across governance domains that are performed in order to support governance for portfolios, programs, and projects. Functions are categorized as oversight, control, integration, and decision making. Refer to Section 3.5 for a summary of domains, functions, and processes.

Portfolio governance guides portfolio management activities in order to optimize investments and achieve organizational strategic goals. These activities determine the actual versus planned aggregated portfolio value to ensure that components deliver maximum return on investment with an acceptable level of risk. As organizational strategic changes occur, governance assesses the impact to the portfolio and determines what adjustments are needed in portfolio goals, plans, and components. Also, as changes are requested in the portfolio goals, strategies, or plans, governance provides the decision-making mechanism to respond to the proposed strategic changes. As changes to portfolio goals, strategies, or plans are being made, continuous strategic alignment may impact the benefits that are planned and delivered.

Portfolio governance provides the framework for making decisions, providing oversight, ensuring controls, and overseeing integration within the portfolio components. Portfolio governance ensures the correct alignment of components to achieve organizational strategy. Portfolio governance is responsible for decisions regarding resources (e.g., human, financial, material, equipment), and ensures alignment to the investment decisions and priorities while any significant organizational constraints are being considered.

Based on the established portfolio authority structure, portfolio governance decision making occurs at various levels of the organization to support specific strategies, goals, and objectives defined through the organization's strategic planning process.

Governance guidance, decision making, and processes may cross organizational and functional management areas of an organization. Portfolio governance guidance and oversight may emanate from organizational governance and multiple governing bodies. In order to be effective, these governing bodies should be linked together to ensure that each decision is aligned with the defined organizational strategy. The governance required should be considered in the context of the portfolio and organizational environment. Portfolio governance should involve the least amount of authority structure possible because time and costs are associated with governance

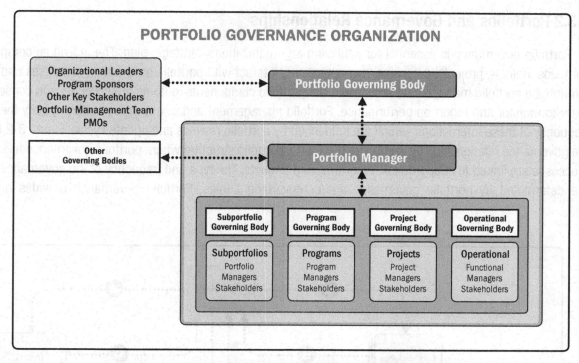

Figure 3-1. Example of Portfolio Governance Organization

decision-making and oversight activities. Figure 3-1 provides an example of a portfolio governance organizational structure that includes portfolio governance with a governing body and provides component governance for each of the subportfolios, programs, projects, and operational teams.

The governing body provides oversight and decision-making support to the portfolio management team and the portfolio manager. Decisions that are made may impact current and future projects and programs within the portfolio. Such impacts include terminating, canceling, or reprioritizing programs or projects within the portfolio. The governing body ensures that the decisions are aligned with organizational strategies. Issues and risks regarding the portfolio performance are escalated to the governing body for required decisions. The governing body ensures that the portfolio goals and investment mix align with organizational strategic and operational goals. Additional governing bodies, such as investment review committees, may exist for subportfolios, programs, projects, and operations in order to provide governance for those specific components.

Portfolio governance processes and activities enable the evaluation of portfolio performance and provide resourcing, investment, and prioritization decisions when needed. The portfolio manager or portfolio management team makes recommendations to the governing body for decisions and guidance. These recommendations may include adding new components, namely, programs and projects, as well as suspending or changing existing components. The portfolio governance coordinates the reporting of portfolio performance and decision making to organizational governing bodies as well as to portfolio management offices, when applicable.

3.3.2 Portfolios and Governance Relationships

Portfolio governance is essential for achieving an organization's strategic plan. The individual components of portfolios, namely, projects, programs, and operations, interact with portfolio governance processes and activities through the portfolio management processes. The portfolio components' outputs are collected and consolidated in order to monitor and report on performance. Portfolio management and/or governing bodies specify the type and frequency of these interactions, which are influenced by portfolio reviews and update cycles. Figure 3-2 illustrates the governance relationships for components within a portfolio structure where portfolio governance functions and processes are linked to subportfolios, programs, and projects. The type and frequency of the governance activities are determined by portfolio governance and/or governing bodies. Portfolio governance provides governance

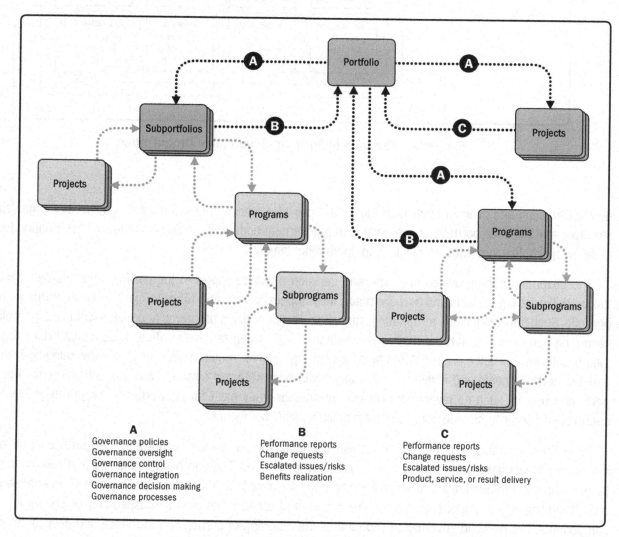

A	B	C
Governance policies	Performance reports	Performance reports
Governance oversight	Change requests	Change requests
Governance control	Escalated issues/risks	Escalated issues/risks
Governance integration	Benefits realization	Product, service, or result delivery
Governance decision making		
Governance processes		

Figure 3-2. Portfolio Governance Relationships

policies, oversight, control, integration, and decision-making functions and processes to subportfolios, programs, and projects within the portfolio structure.

Subportfolios, programs, and projects provide performance reports, change requests, and escalated issues and risks to portfolio governance. Programs provide information on benefits realization, and projects provide information on product, service, or results delivery.

Portfolio managers support governance oversight by reporting on the current performance status of the portfolio through key performance indicator measures and individual portfolio components (i.e., programs and projects). Portfolio managers provide the business impact analysis of changes required to the portfolio, which can be triggered by specific changes (e.g., scope) at the project level or proposed adjustments needed to the portfolio components to meet the target portfolio performance levels. Portfolio governance provides the oversight to ensure that portfolio component performance is trending to achieve the organization's strategic targets. More specifically, portfolio governance provides key decisions regarding the programs and projects within the portfolio.

3.3.3 Portfolio Governance Considerations

Governance occurs at various levels of the organization to support the organizational goals, objectives, and strategies. Organizational strategy and objectives define the means of attaining the goals through operations (business-as-usual activities) or portfolios, programs, and projects. Portfolio governance is a bridge between organizational governance and program and project governance, and operations; as a result, governance levels are linked together to ensure that each governance action is ultimately aligned with the defined organizational strategy.

The portfolio governing body reviews the actual versus targeted performance of the portfolio in order to reach key decisions. This ensures that the portfolio continues to be on track to manage the portfolio risks and to deliver business value and benefits in order to achieve the organization's strategic objectives. As strategic changes occur in the organization, as well as specific portfolio component changes, portfolio governance assesses the impact to the portfolio and determines what adjustments are needed to the portfolio mix. Portfolio governance activities monitor portfolio risks that may impact the financial value of the portfolio, the portfolio component mix used to achieve the organizational strategy and objectives, and the impact to the organization's capacities and capabilities.

Another portfolio governance consideration is the integrated governance processes. Integrated governance processes are a critical component of the governance activities and include strategic alignment, prioritization, and authorization of components and allocation of internal resources to accomplish organizational strategy and objectives.

3.4 Roles and Responsibilities

The key roles for portfolio governance are the governing body; portfolio sponsor; portfolio manager; portfolio, program, and project management office (PMO); program sponsor; program manager; project sponsor; project manager; and functional manager. There may be other responsibilities not included for these roles that relate to management activities. There may be additional roles, depending on the governance framework and organizational structure. The typical governance-related roles and responsibilities are the following:

- **Portfolio governing body.** The portfolio governing body should be a collaborative group of executives representing various portfolio components and operational work with the purpose of supporting the portfolio under its authority by providing guidance through the governance functions. The purpose of this governing body is to make decisions about investments and priorities for the portfolio. The governing body ensures that the portfolio is aligned with the organization's strategy by providing the appropriate oversight, leadership, and decision making. It is important to ensure that the portfolio governing body has the delegated authority and capability to make strategic portfolio decisions from the organization's highest-level governing body.

  o Determine portfolio governance framework to include oversight, decision-making, control, and integration functions (refer to Table 3-1 for portfolio governance processes by domains and functions).

  o Ensure that the portfolio strategic plan aligns with the organizational strategic and operational goals.

  o Approve governance-related policies and processes.

  o Control allocation of resources (human, budgetary, and or facilities) in accordance with an organization's strategic priorities and operational needs.

  o Define key performance targets and thresholds.

  o Establish component selection, categorization, prioritization, and authorization criteria.

  o Provide leadership in making, enforcing, carrying out, and communicating decisions.

  o Influence and direct multiple areas, such as organizational communications, external reporting, funding and investment measures, and strategic direction for new products and services.

  o Provide executive support in portfolio, program, and project process alignment and expectations.

  o Determine the risk and/or reward, including the financial investment, return, and portfolio value.

  o Consider and balance the degree of organizational change required to achieve portfolio value.

  o Review and remediate escalated issues and risks.

  o Review and resolve conflicting goals and objectives.

  o Define key messages to be communicated to stakeholders and the organization.

  o Review performance and proposed recommendations to adjust the portfolio.

- **Portfolio sponsor.** The sponsor's role is to champion the portfolio components, programs, projects, and operations. The sponsor(s) may be members of the governing body. The sponsors are engaged at the portfolio level as well as at the program and project levels and may be contributors to changes and engaged in escalations.

  o Ensure portfolio goals and objectives are aligned with the strategic vision.

○ Monitor and control the portfolio value and delivery of benefits to enable success of the portfolio.

○ Remove barriers and obstacles to portfolio success.

- **Portfolio manager.** The portfolio manager's role is to interface with the governing body and manage the portfolio to ensure that the programs, projects, and operational components deliver the investment benefits and meet the organization's strategic objectives.

  ○ Assess the governance framework including organizational structure, policies, and procedures and, if required, establish the portfolio governance framework.

  ○ Ensure portfolio conformance to governance policies and processes.

  ○ Manage portfolio interactions with the governing body and sponsor.

  ○ Facilitate the selection, prioritization, balancing, and termination of portfolio components to ensure alignment with the strategic goals and organizational priorities.

  ○ Review the portfolio in order to recommend reallocation and reprioritization, and optimize the portfolio to ensure ongoing alignment with evolving organizational goals, opportunities, and threats.

  ○ Provide key stakeholders with timely assessment of portfolio component selection, prioritization, and performance, as well as early identification of (and intervention in) portfolio-level issues and risks that are impacting performance.

  ○ Measure and monitor portfolio value performance metrics and targets such as benefit ratios, return on investment (ROI), net present value (NPV), payback period (PP), internal rate of return (IRR), and scorecards. Government and not-for-profit organizations may have other measures and targets such as productivity and customer satisfaction improvements.

  ○ Support senior-level and governing bodies' decision making by ensuring timely and consistent communication to stakeholders on progress, changes, and impact on portfolio components.

  ○ Participate in program and project reviews to reflect senior-level support, leadership, and involvement in key decisions.

  ○ Assess, report, and escalate critical risks and issues to the governing body.

  ○ Support the program and project managers' assessments of component value in order to deliver component benefits.

  ○ Create, monitor, and communicate the portfolio integrated roadmap and key internal and external dependencies.

- **Program managers.** The program manager's role is to interface with the portfolio manager, governing bodies, and sponsors and to manage the program to ensure delivery of the intended benefits as follows:

  ○ Ensure program conformance to the governance policies and processes.

  ○ Manage program interactions with the portfolio manager, governing body, and sponsor.

- Monitor and manage the program risks, performance, and communications.
- Monitor and report on the overall program funding and health.
- Assess program outcomes and request authorization from the portfolio manager or governing body to change the overall program strategies.
- Assess, report, and escalate critical risks and issues to the portfolio manager and governing body, as appropriate.
- Create, monitor, and communicate the program's integrated roadmap and key internal and external dependencies.
- Manage, monitor, and track the overall program benefits realization.

- **Project managers.** The project manager's role is to interface with the portfolio manager, program manager, and/or project sponsor and manage the delivery of the project's product, service, or result. Ensure project conformance to governance policies and processes.
  - Monitor and manage project risks, performance, and communications.
  - Manage project interactions with the portfolio manager, program manager, governing body, and sponsor.
  - Assess, report, and escalate critical risks and issues to the portfolio manager, program manager, or governing body, as appropriate.
  - Manage the internal and external dependencies for the project.
  - Ensure the engagement of key stakeholders.

- **Other key stakeholders.** Other key stakeholders' roles are to support portfolio organizational and process changes.
  - Support portfolio governance and execution of portfolio components to ensure that defined goals are being met.
  - Support the portfolio governance team to determine the impact of changes.
  - Support any changes impacting the outcome of the programs and projects.
  - Represent the functional area on the governing body, when applicable.
  - Support portfolio governance-related organizational changes.

- **Portfolio management office (PMO).** The role of the PMO may vary depending upon the needs of the organization. The portfolio may have its own PMO or a PMO may support several portfolios. Typically, the PMO supports the portfolio by doing the following:
  - Support the oversight of portfolio components and escalation of issues and risks to the portfolio manager.
  - Support the portfolio by standardizing governance processes and by providing progress information, knowledge sharing, and consolidated reporting.

3.5 Portfolio Governance Domains, Functions, and Processes

The generally recognized processes for portfolio governance are categorized by domains and functions as summarized in Table 3-1. The related functions and processes are grouped into four governance domains: governance alignment, governance risk, governance performance, and governance communications. Processes, activities, and tasks are categorized by the functions of oversight, control, integration, and decision making. These processes are not role specific and pertain to all activities in the governance domains.

The term "generally recognized processes" does not mean that the processes described should be applied uniformly to all portfolios. The organization's leadership is responsible for determining what is appropriate for any given portfolio. In the absence of or immaturity of governance practices, the portfolio manager and sponsor(s) define governance for a given portfolio as detailed in Section 3.6.

Table 3-1. Portfolio Governance Related Processes by Domains and Functions

Functions Domains	Oversight	Control	Integration	Decision Making
Portfolio Governance Alignment Domain	• Create portfolio governance charter • Create portfolio governance management plan • Analyze portfolio, program, and project performance results	• Align portfolios, programs, and projects with organizational strategic goals • Assess portfolio, program, and project management methodology adherence • Conduct portfolio, program, and project reviews • Conduct portfolio strategic alignment annual planning • Identify pipeline, resources, demand/capacity	• Align component mix and roadmaps • Create integrated roadmap with strategy execution tracks • Ensure portfolio, program, and project processes are aligned and integrated • Monitor ongoing changes to portfolios, programs, and projects • Align framework with governing bodies (IT, finance, etc.)	• Determine portfolio component prioritization criteria and funding • Perform go/no-go decisions
Portfolio Governance Risk Domain	• Escalate risks to governing body • Establish risk escalation process • Identify internal/external component dependencies	• Conduct portfolio audits • Manage internal/external resource capacity	• Integrate dependency management • Perform impact analysis of proposed changes • Adjust portfolio based on component changes	• Resolve and remediate risks/issues
Portfolio Governance Performance Domain	• Create performance management plan • Establish reporting and control processes	• Monitor performance regarding investments/value and benefits • Monitor health of portfolio	• Perform integrated performance reporting • Perform benefits realization reporting	• Determine changes to the portfolio based on performance and strategic changes
Portfolio Governance Communications Domain	• Create communications management plan • Communicate portfolio, program, and project governance expectations and requirements • Communicate governance process changes	• Communicate roles, responsibilities, and authorities	• Communicate integrated roadmap • Receive portfolio, program, and project reports	• Report decisions made with justification

The following describes the processes by governance domain:

- **Portfolio governance alignment domain.** To ensure that the proper results from the portfolio are obtained, the governing body should perform periodic reviews of the portfolio as well as additional reviews resulting from escalations requiring decisions. Quarterly and/or annual reviews should be performed to authorize any adjustments or balancing that may be required to ensure alignment to the organizational strategy and confirm objectives.

  - The portfolio governance charter authorizes the formation of the governing body and authorizes the portfolio manager or portfolio management office to apply resources for governance-related activities. The portfolio governance management plan describes how the governance alignment, functions, and processes are to be performed, including governance roles and responsibilities. The plan should be referenced to ensure the portfolio conforms to established agreements and expectations. A governing body (or board or committee) should be established to ensure continuous alignment with organizational strategy and the delivery of the portfolio performance to meet the organization's strategic objectives.

  - The portfolio manager should integrate the portfolio strategy among the portfolio components and ensure that the portfolio is aligned with the organizational strategy. The portfolio should have an integrated roadmap with strategy execution tracks that indicate alignment with business strategy, major events, and dependencies, and that identify which benefits are to be delivered and when. The governing body should approve the integrated roadmap.

  - A governing body (or board or committee) should establish a decision-making framework to review and direct the portfolio investments. The decisions determine the allocation of resources (people and assets) based on strategic goals, risk categories, portfolio objectives, project types, and funding. Based on the decision-making framework and component prioritization criteria, the governing body should determine which program, project, and operational components should be added, changed, or terminated. This framework enables the portfolio manager to balance supply and demand according to the priorities set by the governing body.

- **Portfolio governance risk domain.** Portfolio components should be reviewed and audits performed based on risk and complexity. Escalation processes for risks and performance issues should be defined and communicated. Key dependencies including resources, technical complexity, market opportunity, legal/regulatory risks, and investment thresholds should be identified and monitored closely due to the possible impact on the portfolio performance.

  - The portfolio risk management plan may be a component of the portfolio management plan or may be a separate plan. The plan should include the risk tolerances and reflect the organizational risk policies. The plan should include details defining the escalation processes for risks and issues. Internal and external component dependencies should be identified and monitored closely due to the potential impact on the targeted portfolio performance.

  - Dependency management should include identification of dependencies between portfolio components or with external elements identified within other portfolios. Dependencies should be analyzed and tracked on an ongoing basis.

○ Portfolio-level risks and escalated component risks should be assessed by the portfolio manager and brought to the attention of the governing body for decisions, because there may be broader impacts across the other components in the portfolio as well as the organization. The risks and issues should be included in portfolio reviews and also follow an escalation process that may require decisions from the governing body.

- **Portfolio governance performance domain.** The performance of the portfolio and the impact of the results to the achievement of organizational objectives should be monitored and managed. The portfolio component gate reviews should provide insight on the performance contribution or impact on the portfolio performance and assist with identifying the appropriate actions to take for the portfolio to achieve its performance objectives.

○ The portfolio performance management information may be a component of the portfolio management plan or it may be included in a separate plan. This plan should include the expected performance for the portfolio and ensure that the portfolio delivers the planned benefits that will achieve the organization's strategic objectives. Reporting and control processes should be established and described in the plan.

○ Portfolio components need to be aligned to deliver portfolio benefits. The performance and intended benefits of the portfolio components should be aggregated by reporting to the governing body, sponsor(s), and key stakeholders.

○ The portfolio's ability to deliver the organization's strategic objectives should be continuously monitored and reported. Proposed changes to the portfolio components that may impact achieving the organization's strategic objectives should be evaluated and decided by the governing body.

- **Portfolio governance communications domain.** The governing body, portfolio manager, program manager, project manager, portfolio management office, and sponsor(s) roles, responsibilities, and authorities should be documented and communicated.

○ The portfolio communications management plan may be a component of the portfolio management plan or it may be included in a separate plan. This plan should describe how and when key elements such as component-level risks, performance, and benefits should be reported to the governing body, sponsors, and key stakeholders. The plan should describe how and when various governance decisions are communicated, such as for funding, resources, and changes in the portfolio components.

○ The portfolio roadmap is a key communications vehicle used to indicate how the portfolio components are aligned, whether the order and timing are correct, what benefits are being delivered, and how these elements should be communicated to all stakeholders.

○ Decision making by the governing body should be transparent, documented with justification, and reported to the portfolio stakeholders. Roles, responsibilities, and decision-making authorities should be communicated.

3.6 Portfolio Governance Framework Implementation

Implementation of a governance framework should be based on the maturity and context of the organization. There is no one best governance framework that is effective in all situations. The implementation of portfolio governance should be tailored to the culture and needs of the organization and should leverage existing models of success. This section describes a structured four-step implementation approach, which is summarized in Figure 3-3. The framework implementation is a method for the implementation and continuous improvement of governance processes within a given portfolio management process cycle. The four steps are assess, plan, implement, and improve, with activities and deliverables for each step. All the activities and deliverables may not apply to all portfolios, and there may be other activities and deliverables required based on the organization's size and span of control.

Implementation of portfolio governance is a broad change and the breadth and depth of the portfolio needs to be considered during implementation; therefore, it is important to engage stakeholders on an ongoing basis to help them to understand what the change means for them, to ensure the transition is smooth, and to overcome challenges. This is especially critical when governance is being implemented for the first time. Another essential

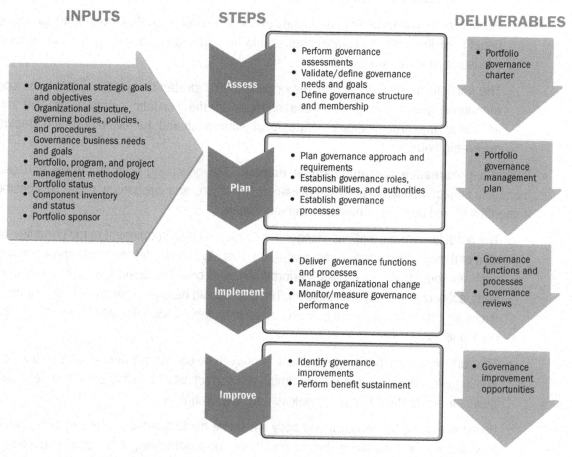

Figure 3-3. Portfolio Governance Framework Implementation

element is ongoing communications to gain stakeholders' support and buy-in for the changes. PMI's *Managing Change in Organizations: A Practice Guide* [5] provides a detailed list of change management models and general guidelines.

Figure 3-4 presents an example of the portfolio governance framework interactions throughout the portfolio management process cycle. These governance interactions depict the effect that the governance framework

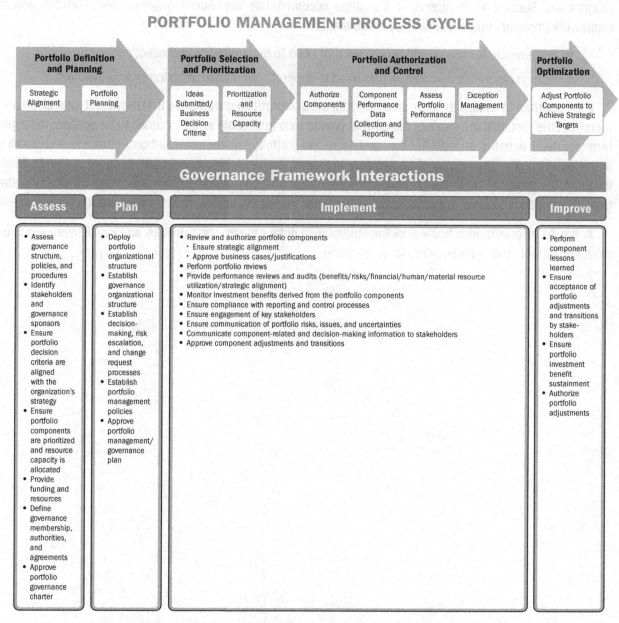

PORTFOLIO MANAGEMENT PROCESS CYCLE

Portfolio Definition and Planning		Portfolio Selection and Prioritization		Portfolio Authorization and Control				Portfolio Optimization
Strategic Alignment	Portfolio Planning	Ideas Submitted/ Business Decision Criteria	Prioritization and Resource Capacity	Authorize Components	Component Performance Data Collection and Reporting	Assess Portfolio Performance	Exception Management	Adjust Portfolio Components to Achieve Strategic Targets

Governance Framework Interactions

Assess	Plan	Implement	Improve

• Assess governance structure, policies, and procedures
• Identify stakeholders and governance sponsors
• Ensure portfolio decision criteria are aligned with the organization's strategy
• Ensure portfolio components are prioritized and resource capacity is allocated
• Provide funding and resources
• Define governance membership, authorities, and agreements
• Approve portfolio governance charter
	• Deploy portfolio organizational structure
	• Establish governance organizational structure
	• Establish decision-making, risk escalation, and change request processes
	• Establish portfolio management policies
	• Approve portfolio management/ governance plan
		• Review and authorize portfolio components
		  • Ensure strategic alignment
		  • Approve business cases/justifications
		• Perform portfolio reviews
		• Provide performance reviews and audits (benefits/risks/financial/human/material resource utilization/strategic alignment)
		• Monitor investment benefits derived from the portfolio components
		• Ensure compliance with reporting and control processes
		• Ensure engagement of key stakeholders
		• Ensure communication of portfolio risks, issues, and uncertainties
		• Communicate component-related and decision-making information to stakeholders
		• Approve component adjustments and transitions
			• Perform component lessons learned
			• Ensure acceptance of portfolio adjustments and transitions by stake-holders
			• Ensure portfolio investment benefit sustainment
			• Authorize portfolio adjustments

Figure 3-4. Portfolio Management Process Cycle and Governance Interactions

implementation has within the portfolio management process cycle. Unlike program and project life cycles, the portfolio is not a phased life cycle that has a defined start and end. Governance should be defined and planned during portfolio definition and planning processes, implemented during the other portfolio process cycles, and improved during optimization. The framework interactions and steps are repeatable due to the nature of portfolio management process cycles.

The governance framework implementation steps may be accomplished in a parallel, overlapping, or linear progression. Successive iterations of the steps accommodate continuous improvement. Portfolio governance framework implementation has two key focus areas:

- Framework, functions, and processes that need to be created or improved; and

- Human resources and culture that need to support governance adoption or improvement.

It is important to assess the current organizational and portfolio governance that may exist for a given portfolio; therefore, the first step is to assess the current governance applicable to the portfolio to be applied; determine the business need, benefits, and justification; and define the portfolio's governance authority structure and membership. In the absence of or immaturity of governance practices, the portfolio manager and sponsor(s) should define and establish the governance for the portfolio early during the portfolio-defining processes when the portfolio strategic plan, charter, and roadmap are created but at the latest during the development of the portfolio management plan.

Annex A1 on governance framework implementation details the inputs, activities, and key deliverables to assess, plan, implement, and improve portfolio governance.

GOVERNANCE AT THE PROGRAM LEVEL

4.1 Overview

This section describes a program and program management; program governance; roles and responsibilities; domains, functions, and processes; and a proposed approach to implement a governance framework within a program life cycle. This section also covers program governance relationships and key considerations. It is recommended that the reader begin by reading Section 1 (Introduction) and then any other sections of interest.

In order to meet organizational strategic and operational goals, program governance is established to provide guidance and oversight of program management activities. Program governance functions and processes are distinct from functional management and managing the work of program components (subprograms, individual projects, and non-project work activities). Program governance focuses on decision making and guidance for program management activities in order to deliver business value to meet organizational strategic and operational goals.

4.2 Program and Program Management

The Standard for Program Management – Third Edition [6] defines a program as "a group of related projects, subprograms, and program activities that are managed in a coordinated way to obtain benefits not available from managing them individually." Programs comprise various components, primarily subprograms and individual projects within the program. Non-project components or program activities are needed to manage the program itself such as training, operations, and maintenance.

The Standard for Program Management – Third Edition defines program management as "the application of knowledge, skills, tools, and techniques to a program to meet the program requirements and to obtain benefits and control not available by managing projects individually." Program management is a function formed to manage, coordinate, and direct the implementation of a set of related projects and activities in order to deliver outcomes and benefits related to the organization's strategic and operational objectives. Program management directs and manages program-related activities and tasks across multiple lines of business, single lines of business, or functional areas within an organization. The program manager manages the interdependencies between program components and the integration of activities to improve strategic alignment and optimize the delivery of benefits. Program management enables appropriate planning, control, delivery, transition, and benefit sustainment across the components in order to achieve the program's intended strategic benefits.

4.3 Program Governance

Program governance is established to provide guidance and oversight of the program management function in order to meet organizational strategic and operational goals. The key difference between program governance and portfolio or project governance is that program governance focuses on guidance to deliver program benefits.

4.3.1 What is Program Governance?

This practice guide defines program governance as the framework, functions, and processes that guide program management activities in order to deliver benefits to meet organizational strategic and operational goals. The term "governance framework" refers to the four governance domains with functions, processes, and activities for portfolios, programs, and projects. Governance functions are a grouping of processes related to each other and across governance domains that are performed in order to support governance for portfolios, programs, and projects. Functions are categorized as oversight, control, integration, and decision making. Examples of governance processes are: establish decision-making process, establish risk escalation process, etc. The highest-level governing body may direct or require that governance processes be established. Refer to Section 4.5 for a summary of domains, functions, and processes.

Program performance and progress information is evaluated through program governance to ensure the program achieves its intended benefits and outcomes. Program governance determines whether benefits achievement is occurring within the stated parameters so component changes can be proposed and executed, when necessary. Program governance coordinates the flow of status reports and performance information to portfolio management, governing bodies, program management offices, program sponsors, and other key program stakeholders. Governance guidance, decision making, and processes may cross organizational and functional management areas as well. Program governance guidance and oversight may be provided by portfolio management, governing bodies, or a program management office based on the organizational structure model, roles, responsibilities, and authorities.

Program governance should involve the least amount of authority structure possible because time and costs are associated with governance decision making and oversight activities. The governance required should be considered in the context of the program and organizational environment. Refer to Figure 4-1 for an example of a program governance organizational structure that includes a program governing body consisting of organizational leaders, program sponsor(s), other key stakeholders, the program management team, and program management offices. This governing body provides oversight and decision-making support to the overall program and program manager. The governing body ensures that program goals and planned benefits align with organizational strategic and operational goals. The other governing bodies (e.g., benefits realization) provide oversight and monitoring so that the program benefits are planned, measured, and achieved. Additional, separate governing bodies may exist to provide guidance for specific subprograms, projects, and operations. The component teams include program and project managers, functional managers, and stakeholders. Programs often authorize and govern subprograms, projects, and operations.

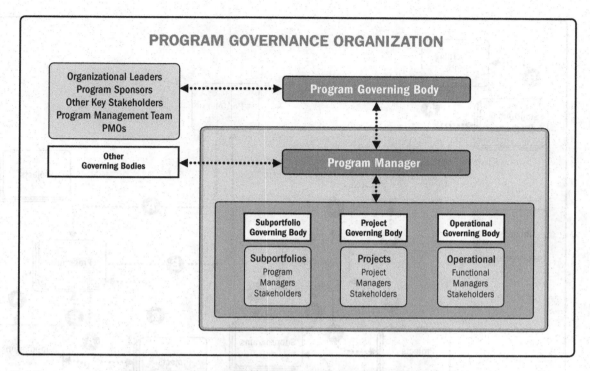

Figure 4-1. Example of Program Governance Organization

4.3.2 Program and Governance Relationships

Programs and governance are interdependent; however, they each have a different purpose. Program components and program activities are managed in a coordinated way to obtain benefits not available by managing them individually. Portfolio governance ensures that the right programs are selected and provides oversight so programs are managed effectively. Ideally, portfolio management and/or governing bodies provide governance guidance for programs and projects. In the absence of or in concert with portfolio governance, program governance should provide guidance and oversight to a program and the program manager.

The individual program components (subprograms, projects, and operations) report and interact through program governance processes on status, risks, changes, and other information affecting the program. The type and frequency of these reports and interactions are specified by portfolio management, governing bodies, and/or program management and are influenced by program reviews and update cycles. Figure 4-2 illustrates the governance relationships for programs within a portfolio structure and outside of a portfolio structure for stand-alone programs. Within a portfolio structure, portfolio governance supporting functions and processes are linked to programs and subprograms through portfolio governance. For stand-alone programs that are outside of a portfolio structure, a governing body provides governance supporting functions and processes to programs. The type and frequency of the governance activities are determined by portfolio governance and/or

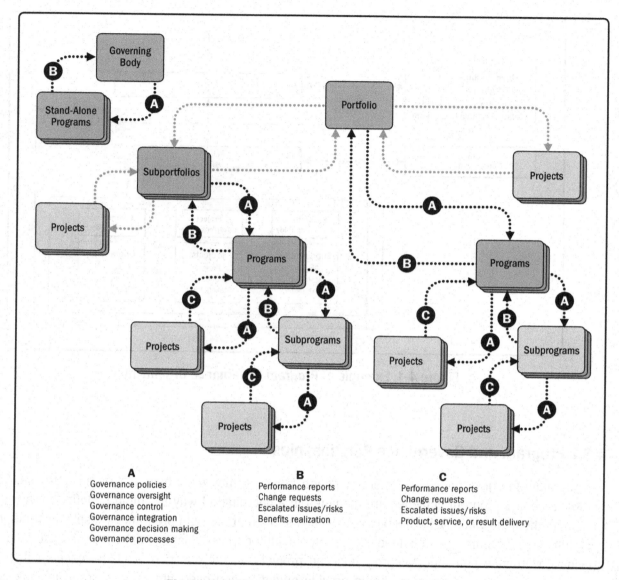

Figure 4-2. Program Governance Relationships

governing bodies. The portfolio and subportfolios provide governance policies, oversight, control, integration, and decision-making functions and processes to programs within the portfolio structure. A governing body should provide governance policies, oversight, control, integration, and decision-making functions and processes to programs that exist outside of a portfolio structure. Refer to Section 4.5 for a summary of domains, functions, and processes. Programs focus on achieving the specific benefits expected while projects are concerned with creating specific deliverables. Programs provide various program reports, change requests, escalated issues and risks, and benefits realization to the portfolio and subportfolio governance and to the governing bodies.

4.3.3 Program Governance Considerations

Strategic alignment, integration management, and benefits realization are three key considerations for program governance. The program manager or team reviews the actual versus planned benefits to ensure alignment with strategic and operational goals. As organizational strategic changes occur, the program manager and/or sponsor assesses the impact to the program and determines what adjustments are needed in program goals, plans, and components. Also, as changes are requested in the program goals, strategies, or plans, program governance provides the decision-making mechanism to respond to the proposed strategic changes. As changes are made to program goals, strategies, or plans, continuous strategic alignment may impact the benefits that were planned and delivered.

Another key consideration for program governance is the oversight of integration management. Integration activities should include strategic alignment of the program goals with organizational strategy and within the program's components, communicated integrated roadmap, integrated dependency management, and integrated performance reporting. Program governance should review the integrated outcomes of subprograms and projects to assess the continued alignment with the intended strategy and the expected delivery of benefits. Integration activities should include coordination and alignment of individual processes (subprograms, projects, and operations) to ensure alignment with the overall program governance processes and to ensure that oversight is provided for escalated issues or risks, effort is not duplicated, and that decision making is provided in a timely manner. Processes should include triggers and thresholds required for corrective or preventive actions.

The delivery of business value through benefits realization is a key area for program governance, which includes benefits delivery, transition, and sustainment. Program governance is critical to support the delivery of benefits expected by the organization. Benefits performance information is evaluated through program governance. Therefore, program governance should provide oversight, control, integration, and decision-making functions to guide benefits realization.

Some program outcomes may be unpredictable, changes in the program may be required, and programs may not have a well-defined ending due to the uncertain timing of the realization of intended benefits; therefore, governance functions are critical due to this ambiguity and due to the need for continual decision making. The extent and rigor of program governance practices may depend upon the nature of the program, its size and complexity, and, foremost, the level of program risk and value to the organization.

4.4 Roles and Responsibilities

The program governance management plan should identify and describe the individual roles and responsibilities including decision-making accountabilities and authorities. The key roles for program governance are outlined below; however, there may be additional roles depending upon the type and complexity of the program and the role of governance. There may be other responsibilities not included for these roles that relate to management activities. The typical governance-related roles and responsibilities include the following:

- **Program governing body.** The program governing body should be a collaborative group of participants representing various program-related interests with the purpose of supporting the program under its authority by providing guidance through the governance functions. The members of the governing body are typically executive-level individuals from the organizational groups that support the program's subprograms, projects, and operations. Typical responsibilities include:

- o Provide governance support for the program to include oversight, control, integration, and decision-making functions (refer to Section 4.5).
- o Provide capable governance resources to oversee and monitor program uncertainty and complexity related to achieving benefits delivery.
- o Ensure program goals and planned benefits align with organizational strategic and operational goals.
- o Establish governance-related policies and processes.
- o Conduct planning sessions to confirm, prioritize, and fund the program.
- o Endorse or approve program recommendations and changes.
- o Define and oversee program gate processes.
- o Resolve and remediate escalated program issues and risks.
- o Provide oversight and monitoring so program benefits are planned, measured, and achieved.
- o Provide leadership in making, enforcing, carrying out, and/or communicating decisions.
- o Define key messages to be communicated to stakeholders.
- o Review expected benefits and benefits delivery.
- o Approve program closure or termination.

- **Program sponsor(s).** The sponsor's role is to champion the program and be accountable for delivering the benefits. The sponsor(s) may be members of the governing body. Typical activities are:
  - o Ensure program goals and objectives are aligned with the strategic vision.
  - o Monitor and control the delivery of benefits to enable success of the program.
  - o Remove barriers and obstacles to program success.

- **Program manager(s).** The program manager's role is to interface with the governing body and sponsor and to manage the program to ensure delivery of the intended benefits as follows:
  - o Assess the governance framework including organizational structure, policies, and procedures and, if required, establish the program governance framework.
  - o Ensure program conformance to governance policies and processes.
  - o Manage program interactions with the governing body and sponsor.
  - o Monitor and manage program risks, performance, and communications.
  - o Monitor and report on overall program funding and health.
  - o Assess program outcomes and request authorization from the governing body to change overall program strategies.
  - o Assess, report, and escalate critical risks and issues to the governing body.

- o Create, monitor, and communicate program integrated roadmap and key internal and external dependencies.

- o Manage, monitor, and track overall program benefits realization.

- **Project managers.** The project manager's role is to interface with the program manager and/or project sponsor and manage the delivery of the project's product, service, or result. Responsibilities include:

  - o Manage project interactions with the program manager, governing body, and sponsor.

  - o Ensure project conformance to governance policies and processes.

  - o Monitor and manage project risks, performance, and communications.

  - o Assess, report, and escalate critical risks and issues to the program manager or governing body, as appropriate.

  - o Manage internal and external dependencies for the project.

  - o Ensure engagement of key stakeholders.

- **Other key stakeholders.** Other key stakeholders' roles are to support program and organizational changes. Stakeholders perform as follows:

  - o Support the program governance team and execution of program components to ensure that defined goals are being met.

  - o Support program governance-related organizational changes.

  - o Support the program governance team to determine the impact of changes.

  - o Support any changes impacting the outcome of the program and components.

  - o Represent the functional area on the governing body, when applicable.

- **Program management office (PMO).** The role of the program management office may vary. The program may have its own PMO, or a PMO may support several programs. Typically, the PMO supports the program by doing the following:

  - o Support the program by standardizing governance processes and by providing progress information, knowledge sharing, and consolidated reporting.

  - o Facilitate the sharing of resources, methodologies, tools, and techniques.

4.5 Program Governance Domains, Functions, and Processes

The generally recognized processes for program governance are categorized by the domains and functions summarized in Table 4-1. The related functions and processes are grouped into four governance domains: governance alignment, governance risk, governance performance, and governance communications. Governance-supporting processes, activities, and tasks are categorized by the functions of oversight, control, integration, and decision making. These processes are not role specific and pertain to all activities in the governance domains.

Table 4-1. Program Governance Related Processes by Domains and Functions

Functions Domains	Oversight	Control	Integration	Decision Making
Program Governance Alignment Domain	• Establish governing body • Create program governance charter • Create program governance management plan	• Manage quality reviews and phase gates • Conduct planning for prioritization and funding	• Integrate program strategy • Create integrated roadmap with strategy execution tracks	• Establish decision-making process • Determine program prioritization and funding • Perform go/no-go decisions for components • Reallocate resources
Program Governance Risk Domain	• Create risk management plan • Establish risk escalation process	• Conduct project audits • Manage program internal/external dependencies	• Integrate dependency management	• Resolve and remediate risks/issues
Program Governance Performance Domain	• Create performance management plan • Establish reporting and control processes	• Monitor benefits realization • Monitor program and component health	• Perform integrated performance reporting	• Assess changes to benefits realization • Assess changes based on performance and strategic changes
Program Governance Communications Domain	• Create communications management plan	• Communicate roles, responsibilities, and authorities	• Communicate integrated roadmap • Disseminate consolidated program reporting • Disseminate program information and impacts to stakeholders	• Report decisions made with justification

Generally recognized processes do not mean that the processes described should be applied uniformly to all programs. The organization's leadership is responsible for determining what is appropriate for any given program. In the absence of or immaturity of governance practices, the program manager and sponsor(s) should define governance for a given program as detailed in Section 4.6.

The following describes the processes by domain:

- **Program governance alignment domain.** The program governance charter recommends the governance organizational structure and describes a high-level program governance approach in order to meet organizational strategic and operational goals. The governance charter may be separate or part of the program charter. The program governance management plan may be a component of the program management plan or may be a separate plan. The plan describes how the governance framework, functions, and processes will be performed including governance roles and responsibilities. The plan should be referenced to ensure the program is conforming to established agreements and expectations.

  ○ A governing body (or board or committee) should be established to ensure continuous alignment with organizational strategy and the delivery of program benefits. Quarterly and/or annual planning should be performed to prioritize the program components in order to align with organizational strategy and to establish the related funding approach. The governing body should manage the program phase gates and other governance reviews such as program quality reviews. The governing body should establish a decision-making framework (rules and procedures) and determine the prioritization of resources (people and assets) based on strategic goals, risk categories, project types, and funding.

Based on the decision-making framework and prioritization criteria, the governing body should determine which program components will be added, changed, or terminated or determine whether the program itself should be changed or terminated. The governing body should make go/no-go decisions and reallocate resources based on those decisions.

○ The program manager should integrate the program strategy among the components and ensure the program is aligned with organizational strategy. The program should have an integrated roadmap with strategy execution tracks that indicate alignment with organizational strategy, major events, and dependencies and identify which benefits are to be delivered and when. The governing body should approve the integrated roadmap.

- **Program governance risk domain.** The program governance risk management plan may be a component of the program management plan or may be a separate plan. Escalation processes for risks and issues should be included in the plan, established, and communicated. The risks and issues should be included in program reviews and also follow the risk/issue escalation processes. The program and components should be monitored and audited based on risk and complexity. Internal/external dependencies should be monitored closely due to the potential impact to benefits delivery. Program-level risks and escalated component risks should be assessed by the program manager and brought to the attention of the sponsor and governing body for decisions as there may be broader impacts across the organization. Dependency management should include identification of dependencies between program components or with external elements. Dependencies should be analyzed and tracked on an ongoing basis.

- **Program governance performance domain.** The program governance performance management information may be a component of the program management plan and/or the benefits management plan. The plan should include expected performance and benefits to ensure that the program delivers the planned benefits. Reporting and control processes should be established and described in the plan.

○ The full benefits life cycle (identification, planning, delivery, transition, and sustainment) should be monitored and managed as well as the overall health of the program and critical, high-priority components. Performance data should be evaluated to ensure results are within parameters. The governing body should monitor the delivery of benefits through performance reviews. The program's ability to deliver benefits should be continuously monitored and reported. Proposed changes to the program that may impact benefits realization should be evaluated and determined by the governing body.

○ Program components need to be integrated to deliver benefits. The performance and intended benefits of program components should be integrated by means of reporting to the governing body, sponsor(s), and key stakeholders.

- **Program governance communications domain.** The program governance communications management plan may be a component of the program management plan or may be a separate plan. The plan should describe how and when elements such as program-level risks, performance, and benefits should be reported to the governing body, sponsor, and key stakeholders. Effective governance determines and allocates clear decision rights; therefore, the governing body; program manager; and sponsor's roles, responsibilities, and authorities should be documented and communicated to all stakeholders. The plan should describe how and when various governance decisions are communicated, such as funding, resources, and changes in the program. Decision making by governance should be transparent, documented with justification, and reported to stakeholders.

- ○ The program integrated roadmap is a key communications vehicle used to indicate how the components are aligned, whether the order and timing are correct, what benefits are being delivered, and how these elements should be communicated to all stakeholders. Program information such as status, policies, procedures, and processes impacting other portfolios, programs, and projects should be communicated to stakeholders.

4.6 Program Governance Framework Implementation

Implementation of program governance should be based on the context of the organization and program. There is no one best program governance implementation approach that would be effective in all situations. The implementation of governance should be tailored to the culture of the organization, types of projects, and needs of the organization. This section describes a structured four-step implementation approach, which is summarized in Figure 4-3. The governance framework implementation approach is a method for the implementation and

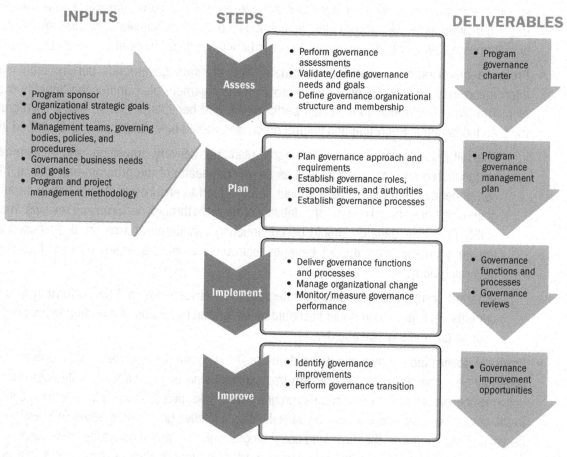

Figure 4-3. Program Governance Framework Implementation

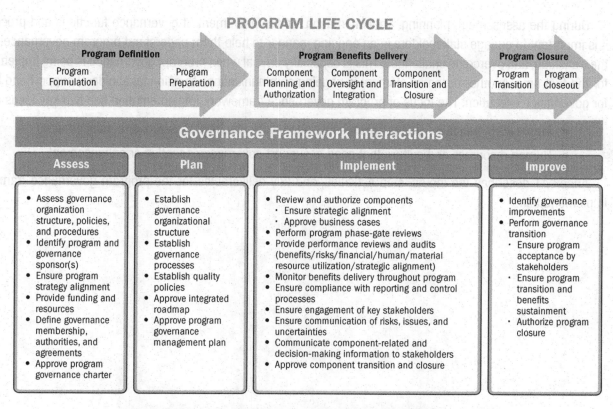

Figure 4-4. Program Life Cycle and Governance Interactions

continuous improvement of governance processes within a given program life cycle. The four steps are assess, plan, implement, and improve, with activities for each step and deliverables. All the activities and deliverables may not apply to all programs, and there may be other activities and deliverables required based on the program scope and organizational context.

Figure 4-4 presents an example of program governance framework interactions by program life cycle phase. These interactions depict the effect that the governance framework implementation has within the program life cycle. A generic program life cycle as detailed in *The Standard for Program Management* – Third Edition has three phases: program definition, program benefits delivery, and program closure. The governance framework implementation steps are indicated within the program life cycle by program life cycle phase. Governance should be defined, planned, and established in the program life cycle definition phase, implemented during the program benefits delivery phase, and improved during the program closure phase. The framework interactions are iterative during the program benefits delivery phase due to the iterations of component authorization, transition, and closure.

To initiate the assess step, inputs may include a variety of elements as indicated in Figure 4-3. A structured approach to implement or enhance governance functions and processes should add business value to the business unit or the organization.

During the assessment, planning, implementation, and improvement of governance functions and processes, it is important to engage stakeholders in an ongoing manner to help them understand program governance, make the transition, and overcome challenges. This is especially critical when program governance is being implemented for the first time. Another essential element is ongoing communications to gain stakeholders' support and buy-in for governance execution. The focus of program governance framework implementation has two key focus areas:

- Framework, functions, and processes that need to be identified, created, or enhanced; and

- Human resources and culture that need to support governance adoption or enhancement.

Annex A1 describes the inputs, step activities, and key deliverables for the program governance framework implementation.

5

GOVERNANCE AT THE PROJECT LEVEL

5.1 Overview

This section describes a project and project management; project governance; roles, and responsibilities; domains, functions, and processes; and a proposed approach to implement a governance framework within a project life cycle. This section also covers project governance relationships and key considerations. It is recommended that the reader begin by reading Section 1 (Introduction) and then any other sections of interest.

In order to meet organizational strategic and operational goals, project governance is established to provide guidance and oversight of project management activities. Project governance focuses on guidance and decision making for project management activities in order to create a service, product, or result.

5.2 Project and Project Management

A Guide to the Project Management Body of Knowledge (PMBOK® Guide) – Fifth Edition [7] defines a project as "a temporary endeavor undertaken to create a unique product, service, or result." A project contains a series of activities aimed at meeting customer needs within a defined time period and requires participation of various stakeholders in order to create a unique product, service, or result with specific scope, time, cost, and performance requirements.

Project management, as defined in the PMBOK® Guide – Fifth Edition, defines project management as "the application of knowledge, skills, tools, and techniques to project activities to meet the project requirements." Project management contains the Initiating, Planning, Executing, Monitoring and Controlling, and Closing Process Groups. Each Process Group has specific process outputs. Project management activities are managed according to the scope, time, and budget requirements in order to deliver a product, service, or result.

5.3 Project Governance

The key difference between project governance and portfolio or program governance is that project governance focuses on the guidance and oversight for project management activities in order to deliver a product, service, or result. In addition to this practice guide, the PMBOK® Guide – Fifth Edition provides additional information on the project management context.

5.3.1 What is Project Governance?

This practice guide defines project governance as the framework, functions, and processes that guide project management activities in order to create a unique product, service, or result and meet organizational strategic and operational goals. Governance framework refers to the four governance domains (oversight, control, integration, and decision making) with functions, processes, and activities for portfolios, programs, and projects. Governance functions are a grouping of processes related to each other and across governance domains that are performed in order to support governance for portfolios, programs, and projects. Functions are categorized as oversight, control, integration, and decision making. Refer to Section 5.5 for a summary of domains, functions, and processes.

The competing objectives of the project triple constraint (time, cost, and scope) make the execution of a project challenging. Because of these challenges, project governance is needed to guide and oversee the management of project execution and to ensure appropriate stakeholder engagement.

The business environment changes every day; therefore, in this dynamic environment, project governance should guide inputs, validation of project and product requirements, effective execution, and the quality of the results. This guidance should be achieved by appropriate involvement in projects and interactions with the project manager on a regular basis. The project governing body should champion the project within the organization by getting the appropriate people involved. Project governance should involve the least amount of authority structure possible because time and costs are associated with governance decision-making and oversight activities.

The project governance requirements should be considered in the context of the project and organizational environment. A project may be governed in three separate scenarios: as a stand-alone project, within a program, or within a portfolio. Figure 5-1 shows an example of a project governance organizational structure that

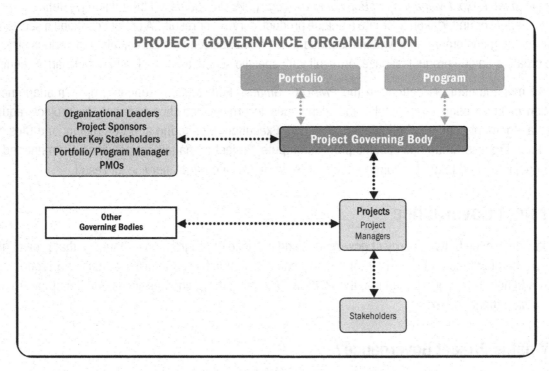

Figure 5-1. Example of Project Governance Organization

includes project governance considering the three scenarios. Project governance has interactions with portfolio and program governance when the project is within a portfolio or program. However, when the project is a stand-alone project (outside of a portfolio or program), it may have a separate governing body. Organizational leaders, project sponsor, portfolio/program manager, PMO, or other key stakeholders may be members of the project governing body. This governing body has interactions with the project and project manager and with stakeholders.

There are also project governance functions or activities to monitor and report on a project's delivery of a product, service, or defined result. The project governing body determines whether delivery of the product, service, or result is occurring within stated conditions. The project manager coordinates the flow of status reports and performance information to portfolio management, program management, governing bodies, PMOs, project sponsors, and other project key stakeholders as the scenario dictates and based on the agreed-upon interaction requirements.

5.3.2 Projects and Governance Relationships

Each project has unique characteristics in terms of uncertainty, complexity, and risk levels that affect how a project is managed and governed. Project governance provides guidance to project managers, sponsors, and key stakeholders for all types of projects within the organization.

A project governance framework provides the project manager and team with structure, processes, decision-making models, and tools for managing the project, while supporting and controlling the project for successful delivery. Project governance has interactions with a project by means of processes, decision-making models, tools, procedures, and documented policies.

Project governance should establish transparency and confidence in decision making and clarify roles and responsibilities that impact the success of a project. The project governance guidance and information flow from portfolio management, program management, and/or governing bodies to projects. Projects report and interact through project governance processes on status, risks, changes, deliverables, and other information affecting the project. Figure 5-2 illustrates how portfolios, programs, subportfolios, and subprograms interact with project governance. Project governance relationships may include three different project scenarios: stand-alone projects, projects within a program, or projects within a portfolio. Governance policies, oversight, control, integration, decision making, and processes flow down from the governing body to the project in each scenario. Performance reports; change requests; escalated highest-level issues and risks; and product, service, or result delivery flow up to the governing body in each scenario.

Typically, the entire organization interacts with projects, either directly or indirectly. Governance affects how the project is managed. Project governance guidance and oversight may come from the governing bodies; portfolio and program management; and/or a portfolio, program, or project management office, based on the organizational structure, roles, responsibilities, and authorities.

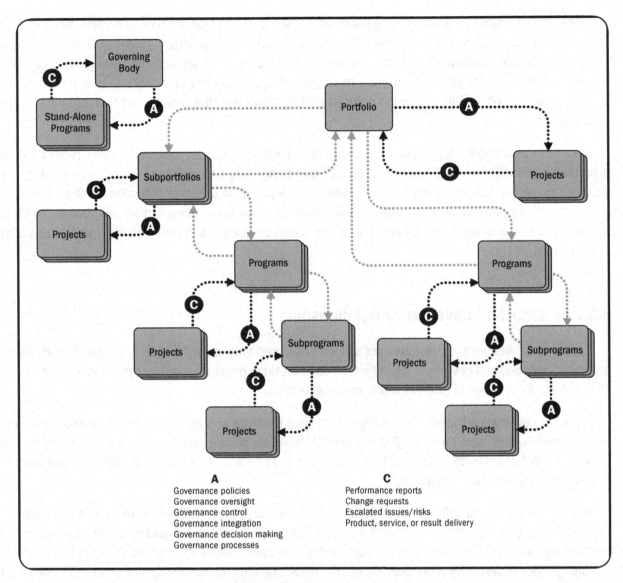

Figure 5-2. Project Governance Relationships

5.3.3 Project Governance Considerations

Project governance enables a disciplined approach for project management and improves opportunities for project success. The primary project governance considerations concern the project governing body and sponsor as follows:

- **Involvement of the governing body and sponsor.** The governing body should be actively involved in providing oversight and decision making for the project. The governing body should ensure that phase-gate processes are followed, strategic alignment is maintained, and significant or escalated risks and issues are reviewed and mitigated. The sponsor should champion the project by being involved in various key activities and processes to ensure success of the project. The sponsor should identify and monitor the project's critical success factors and be proactive with regard to eliminating or mitigating barriers to the project's success. In some instances, the sponsor may be part of the governing body or the sponsor may be the only individual to provide governance guidance and oversight.

- **Provision of (organizational) functional expertise and/or support.** The governing body or sponsor should ensure appropriate management and resources to provide organizational and/or functional expertise in order to support project execution. This expertise and support may not be provided directly by the governing body itself but by a representative assigned by the governing body or sponsor.

- **Implementation of organizational change management.** The governing body and sponsor should support organizational change management as outlined in *Managing Change in Organizations: A Practice Guide*. Organizational change support is critical for project success, and any organizational change should be assessed and implemented carefully. Organizational changes and their impact to strategy execution should be addressed by the governing body and sponsor. To effectively manage change in projects, the governing body and sponsor ensures that a change management structured approach is followed for transitioning individuals, groups, and organizations from the current state to a future state with intended business benefits. The sponsor deals with the business issues associated with the change to ensure that the benefits of the change are achieved. The sponsor works with the project manager to identify the change management and transition activities and resources required. The sponsor also supports and builds commitment for the project across the organization. The sponsor should ensure that any conflicts are resolved in an appropriate manner.

- **Authority and capability of the governing body and sponsor.** The governing body and sponsor should have the required authority and capability to guide project management and be actively involved in the project. The useful effects of active involvement may be very limited unless the governing body and sponsor have the necessary capability. The decision-making structure may not be successful if the governing body and sponsor do not have the required authority. The capabilities of the sponsor and governing body may include: anticipate change, generate confidence, initiate action, liberate thinking, and evaluate results.

5.4 Roles and Responsibilities

The key project governance roles are project governing body, project sponsor, project manager, other key stakeholders, and the project management office. There may be additional roles depending upon the type and complexity of the project and the role of governance. The project governance management plan should identify and describe the individual roles and responsibilities including decision-making accountabilities and authorities. The governance-related roles and responsibilities include the following:

- **Project governing body.** The project governing body provides oversight, sets direction, and ensures that the project remains aligned with the organization's strategic goals and objectives. Project governing body members are typically executive-level individuals from the organizational groups that support the projects. This body mainly provides guidance through the functions of oversight, control, integration, and decision making. The primary roles and responsibilities of a project governing body may include:

- o Provide governance support for the project to include oversight, control, integration, and decision-making functions (refer to Section 5.5).
- o Establish governance policies and processes.
- o Ensure that project goals align with organizational strategic and operational goals.
- o Endorse or approve project recommendations and changes.
- o Define and oversee project-gating processes.
- o Resolve and remediate escalated project issues and risks.
- o Define key messages to be communicated to stakeholders.
- o Provide capable governance resources to oversee and monitor the project's uncertainty and complexity related to achieving the expected product, service, or result.
- o Provide oversight and guidance so the project team plans, measures, and achieves the product, service, or result.
- o Provide leadership in enforcing, carrying out, and/or communicating decisions.
- o Approve project closure or termination.

- **Project sponsor.** The project sponsor provides resources required for the project to deliver the intended results. The sponsor may be a member of the governing body. The sponsor's active and visible support of project governance is important to enable success of the project. The main roles and responsibilities of the project sponsor are as follows:

- o Ensure project goals and objectives are aligned with the strategic vision.
- o Monitor and control the delivery of the product, service, or result to enable success of the project.
- o Remove barriers and obstacles to project success.

- **Project manager.** The project manager supports the governance functions and processes and coordinates communications as well as provides feedback for improvement to the governance process. The project manager's role is to interface with the governing body and manage the project to ensure delivery of the intended results. The project manager helps ensure that the project is in compliance with governance policies and adheres to the governance processes. The project manager's main roles and responsibilities are as follows:

- o Assess the governance framework including organizational structure, policies, and procedures and, when required, establish the project governance framework.
- o Ensure project conformance to governance policies and processes.
- o Manage project interactions with the governing body and sponsor.

○ Monitor and manage project risks, performance, and communications.

○ Assess, report, and escalate critical risks and issues to the sponsor and/or governing body, as appropriate.

○ Manage internal and external dependencies for the project.

○ Ensure engagement of key stakeholders.

- **Other key stakeholders.** Other key stakeholders are active proponents and supporters of project governance and should represent their areas of the project. Other stakeholders are the people directly or indirectly impacted by the project governance processes and functions such as project team members, functional managers, etc. Their input into the governance process is also important. The main roles and responsibilities of key stakeholders are as follows:

○ Support the project governance team and project execution to ensure that defined goals are being met.

○ Support project governance-related organizational changes.

○ Support the project governance team to determine the impact of changes.

○ Support any changes impacting the outcome of the project.

○ Represent the functional area on the governing body, when applicable.

- **Project management office (PMO).** The PMO role may vary for different types of projects. The PMO is typically responsible for ensuring that project governance standards and processes are implemented effectively and for providing feedback for improvement to the governance process. The main roles and responsibilities of the PMO are as follows:

○ Support the project by standardizing governance processes and by providing progress information, knowledge sharing, and consolidated reporting.

○ Facilitate the sharing of resources, methodologies, tools, and techniques.

5.5 Project Governance Domains, Functions, and Processes

This section provides domains, functions, and processes that will help guide practitioners and organizations in the implementation of governance for projects. Projects have different levels of uncertainty, complexity, and risk, which make it impossible to have one governance framework that fits all projects. A detailed integrative practice and technique may guide one practitioner; however, the same integrative practice and technique may not work for another practitioner because organizational environments are unique. This section utilizes a general categorization by domains, functions, and processes that can be tailored to any specific project as outlined in Table 5-1. The related functions and processes are grouped into four governance domains: governance alignment, governance risk, governance performance, and governance communications. Governance supporting processes, activities, and tasks are categorized by the functions of oversight, control, integration, and decision making. These processes are not role specific and pertain to all activities in the governance domains.

Table 5-1. Project Governance Related Processes by Domains and Functions

Functions Domains	Oversight	Control	Integration	Decision Making
Project Governance Alignment Domain	• Create project governance charter • Create project governance management plan • Establish governing body	• Monitor the adherence to governance management plan • Conduct project reviews and phase-gate reviews • Assess project management methodology adherence	• Integrate project governance into program and/or portfolio governance • Ensure project processes are aligned	• Establish decision-making process • Approve phase-gate reviews • Approve project schedule, scope, and budget
Project Governance Risk Domain	• Create risk management plan • Establish risk escalation process	• Conduct project audits • Ensure risk management adherence • Manage the project's internal and/or external dependencies	• Integrate dependency management • Perform impact analysis of proposed change	• Resolve and remediate escalated risks and issues • Identify, review, and mitigate risks
Project Governance Performance Domain	• Create performance management plan • Establish reporting and control processes • Analyze project performance results	• Monitor project results • Monitor project health	• Perform performance reporting	• Assess proposed changes • Assess change requests
Project Governance Communications Domain	• Create communication management plan • Communicate governance expectations and requirements • Communicate governance process changes • Champion organizational changes and ensure implementation acceptance	• Communicate roles, responsibilities, and authorities	• Communicate roadmap • Disseminate project reporting • Disseminate project information and impacts to stakeholders	• Report decisions made with justification

The following describes the processes by domain:

- **Project governance alignment domain.** The project governance alignment domain consists of the following:

   o The project governance charter authorizes the formation of the governing body and authorizes the governing body to apply resources to implement governance-related activities. The project governance management plan describes how the governance framework, functions, and processes will be performed including governance roles, responsibilities, and decision-making structures. The plan should be referenced to ensure the project is conforming to established agreements and expectations.

   o A project governing body should be established to ensure continuous alignment with organizational strategy and the delivery of project results. The project manager is also responsible for the project's adherence to the governance framework. The project management office, when it exists, is responsible for integration of project governance with portfolio/program governance. Moreover, it is important to monitor the adherence to the project governance management plan. A governing body should establish a decision-making framework and determine who will make what kind of decisions and in what scenarios. Based on the decision-making framework, the governing body should determine if the project should be changed or terminated.

- o To monitor and ensure alignment, the governing body provides guidance and decision making for project schedule, scope, and budget as well as oversees project reviews, phase gates, and adherence to policies, standards, and project management methodology.

- **Project governance risk domain.** The project governance risk management plan is prepared as a part of the project management plan or may be a separate plan. Escalation processes for risks and issues should be established and included in this plan. Internal and external dependencies as well as the risks should be identified. Dependency management should include identification of dependencies between projects or with programs and/or portfolios and other external elements. Dependencies should be analyzed and tracked on an ongoing basis since they are sources of risks. Projects should be monitored and audited based on risk and complexity. Internal and external dependencies should also be monitored. In order to resolve and remediate risks and/or issues, the project manager should escalate decisions to the governing body, as there may be broader impacts across the organization. The risks and/or issues should be included in project reporting and reviews, and should also follow risk and issue escalation processes.

- **Project governance performance domain.** The project governance performance management plan is prepared as a part of the project management plan or may be a separate plan. The plan should include expected performance to ensure the project delivers the expected result. As a part of this plan, the reporting structure and control processes can be established. It is also important to provide performance reporting to the governing body, sponsor, project management office, and key stakeholders. This is one of the key domains that enable the project manager to collect necessary data for performance measurement. The governing body should monitor the performance of projects as outlined in the performance management plan through performance reviews. Performance data should be evaluated to ensure results are within the plan parameters. The project's ability to deliver results should be continuously monitored and reported. Proposed changes to the project that may impact project results should be evaluated and determined by the governing body.

- **Project governance communications domain.** The project governance communications management plan is prepared as a part of the project management plan or may be a separate plan. The plan should describe how and when elements such as project-level risks, performance, and project results should be reported to the governing body, sponsor, and key stakeholders. The plan should describe how and when various governance decisions are communicated and should include how to get feedback from key stakeholders. The governing body should provide required communication to the project manager, sponsor, project management office, and key stakeholders. The governing body should monitor communication based on the communications management plan and take actions to improve communication. Decision making by governance should be transparent, documented with justification, and reported to stakeholders. Roles, responsibilities, and decision-making authorities should be communicated.

5.6 Project Governance Framework Implementation

Implementation of a project governance framework should be based on the context of the organization and project. There is no one governance framework that is effective in all situations. The implementation of a governance framework should be tailored to the culture of the organization, the types of projects, and the needs of the organization. This section describes a structured, four-step implementation approach, which is summarized in Figure 5-3. The implementation approach is a method for the implementation and continuous improvement of governance processes within a given project life cycle. The four steps are: assess, plan, implement, and improve, with activities and deliverables for each step. All the activities and deliverables may not apply to all projects, and there may be other activities and deliverables required based on the project scope and organizational context.

The steps to implement or enhance governance are those used to implement any process in an organization. A structured approach to implement or enhance governance functions and processes should add business value to the business unit or at the organizational level. These steps may be accomplished in a parallel, overlapping,

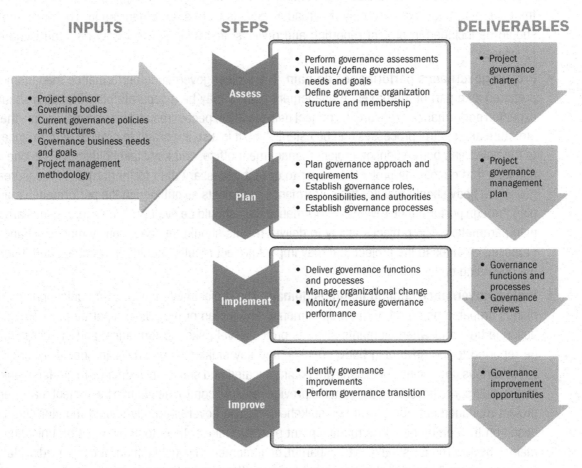

Figure 5-3. Project Governance Framework Implementation

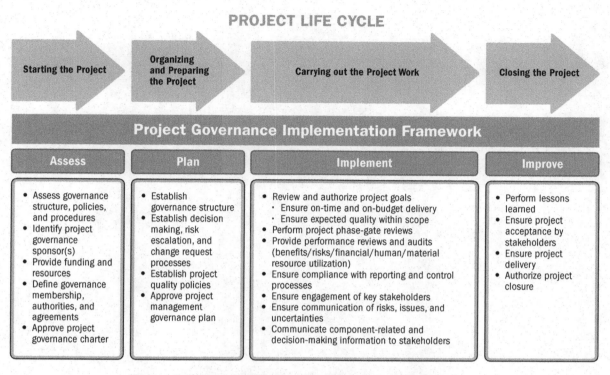

Figure 5-4. Project Life Cycle and Governance Interactions

or linear progression. However, governance should be defined, planned, and established early in the project life cycle when starting, organizing, and preparing for the project.

During the assessment, planning, implementation, and improvement of governance functions and processes, it is important to engage stakeholders on an ongoing basis to help them understand what the change means for them, make the transition, and overcome challenges. This is especially critical when governance is being implemented for the first time. Another essential element is ongoing communications to gain stakeholders' support and buy-in for the changes.

Figure 5-4 presents an example of project governance framework interactions by project life cycle phase. These interactions depict the effect the governance framework implementation has within the project life cycle. A generic project life cycle as detailed in the *PMBOK® Guide* – Fifth Edition has four phases: start the project, organize and prepare the project, carry out the project work, and close the project. The governance framework implementation enables these interactions so that a project can be guided by governance during its life cycle.

Annex A1 on project governance framework implementation details the inputs, activities, and key deliverables to assess, plan, implement, and improve project governance.

REFERENCES

[1] Project Management Institute. 2014. *Navigating Complexity: A Practice Guide.* Newtown Square, PA: author.

[2] Project Management Institute. 2014. *Implementing Organizational Project Management: A Practice Guide.* Newtown Square, PA: author.

[3] Project Management Institute. 2013. *Organizational Project Management Maturity Model (OPM3®) –* Third Edition. Newtown Square, PA: author.

[4] Project Management Institute. 2013. *The Standard for Portfolio Management – Third Edition.* Newtown Square, PA: author.

[5] Project Management Institute. 2013. *Managing Change in Organizations: A Practice Guide.* Newtown Square, PA: author.

[6] Project Management Institute. 2013. *The Standard for Program Management –* Third Edition. Newtown Square, PA: author.

[7] Project Management Institute. 2013. *A Guide to the Project Management Body of Knowledge (PMBOK® Guide) –* Fifth Edition. Newtown Square, PA: author.

ANNEX A1
PORTFOLIO, PROGRAM, AND PROJECT GOVERNANCE FRAMEWORK IMPLEMENTATION

The purpose of this annex is to provide guidance on portfolio, program, and project governance framework implementation details in order to assess, plan, implement, and improve governance.

A1.1 Portfolio Governance Framework Implementation Steps

The implementation steps for a portfolio governance framework are provided in Sections A1.1.1 through A1.1.4 (see also Figure A1-1).

A1.1.1 Assess

As a first step, it is important to understand the current state of the portfolio's governance and processes. An important note is that portfolios are ongoing and longer range than programs and projects; therefore, periodic assessments may be needed. Performing an assessment in various areas of the organization along with the governance business needs helps to identify the target state and gaps and determine the portfolio governance scope, organizational structure, hierarchy, and roles in order to develop a portfolio governance charter.

The portfolio sponsor and portfolio manager should initiate the assessment for portfolio governance when there are no existing governance framework, functions, and processes or the current governance processes may need to be reengineered or improved to progress to the next level of effectiveness. To initiate the assess step, the key inputs are:

- Organizational strategic goals and objectives;
- Organizational structure, governing bodies, policies, and procedures;
- Governance business needs and goals;
- Portfolio, program, and project management methodology;
- Portfolio status;
- Component inventory and status; and
- Portfolio sponsor.

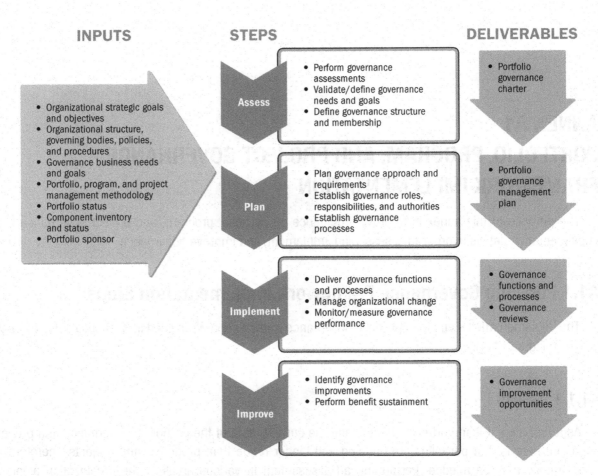

Figure A1-1. Portfolio Governance Framework Implementation

The extent of the assessment depends on the functions or processes that need to be implemented or improved and/or resources or culture and behavior change that needs to support governance. Organizations commonly use surveys, interviews, or meetings and focus groups to gather the information necessary to analyze the current governance environment and perform various analyses. The analyses are necessary to determine the gap between current state and desired future state. The assessment determines *who*, *what*, and *how* of governance and what is required to fill the gaps in order to successfully implement governance. The analysis should uncover who is making the investment decisions, what the authorities and decision areas or boundaries are, and how these decisions are being made and communicated. The assessment activities should encompass the following areas:

- **Perform stakeholder analysis.** Determine the current accountabilities and decision authorities. Then identify and engage key stakeholders to define governance needs, benefits, and justification for portfolio governance. Engage stakeholders to understand the culture, politics, and concerns to determine how these may impact strategic alignment and investment optimization. Identify influencers such as other portfolio or organizational complexity, politics, culture, and external stakeholders.

- **Perform governance assessments.** Determine what may impact the success of governance planning and implementation. Understand the organization's strategy and assess the strategic alignment process. Determine if the current process ensures optimization and portfolio alignment with organizational strategic objectives and investment optimization. Determine how alignment will occur within the portfolio components to support organizational strategic goals. The findings should support the implementation of or enhancement to the portfolio governance framework, functions, and processes. The following areas should be assessed:

  o *Understand organizational governance policies and structures.* Assess if the current organizational structures and policies facilitate the appropriate portfolio governance mechanisms for the selection of projects that ensure achievement of the organization's goals and delivery of business value.

  o *Understand organizational mission, goals, and objectives.* Understand the organization's strategic goals and objectives and how portfolio strategic alignment occurs. Assess the portfolio alignment process and determine if the current process ensures the appropriate project selection that is aligned with strategic goals and program and project delivery of business benefits.

  o *Determine decision making and authorities.* Understand how investment decisions are made and who is making these decisions. Assess the current areas and the scope of decision making, specific authorities, roles and responsibilities, as well as related communications. Determine any issues with decision making and potential causes of the issues.

  o *Determine portfolio oversight capability and controls.* Understand and assess the existing processes and controls that enable portfolio governance oversight, such as investment reviews, portfolio component phase gates, and resource allocation.

  o *Evaluate portfolio, program, and project management resources and competency.* Assess the skills and capabilities as well as the competencies of sponsors and key stakeholders who need to support portfolio governance.

  o *Determine communications and level of transparency.* Assess and determine the effectiveness of what is being communicated and to whom with regard to portfolio governance and, in particular, the investment decisions.

  o *Evaluate culture for governance adoption.* Determine the readiness for change based on the history of change adoption, lessons learned, and both previous and current issues.

  o *Determine strategic key performance indicators (KPIs).* Assess what KPIs are being used to support current portfolio governance oversight, such as portfolio phase-gate reviews.

  o *Evaluate integration of governance for portfolios, programs, and projects.* Assess how resources are allocated and how the processes align across the portfolio management domain.

  o *Perform gap analysis.* Perform a gap analysis of the current state to the future state to provide insight on the assessment areas that have existing gaps. This will facilitate the ability to perform a risk analysis against the gap and prioritize the work to be performed in order to achieve the future state.

o *Perform SWOT/risk analyses.* Analyze the strengths, weaknesses, opportunities, and threats to strategic alignment and benefits realization. Determine the impacts of identified risks to the attainment of portfolio goals and business benefits. Determine how the rollout of governance-related functions and processes would improve strategic alignment and benefits realization.

- **Validate/define governance needs and goals.** Based on the governance assessments and analyses, validate/define portfolio governance needs and goals. Governance needs and goals are unique to an organization and to the individual portfolio. Sponsors and key stakeholders may provide direction for governance needs, goals, organizational structure, membership, and authorities. Examples of governance needs and goals are decision-making transparency, accountability, risk management, etc. The portfolio governance plan should describe the governance goals and various decision and prioritization criteria and authorities in areas such as portfolio changes, phase-gate reviews, component initiation and transition, and resolution of escalated issues and risks.

- **Define governance organizational structure and membership.** Based on stakeholder analysis, various assessments, SWOT/risk analyses, and the approved portfolio objectives, define the portfolio's required governance organizational structure and membership. The organizational structure should be based on the needs of the organization and the portfolio's requirements. The organizational structure and members may be different for the portfolio governance versus the subportfolio and component governance. Document in detail the organizational structure, members, and roles, and how the organizational structure and membership changes during the selection and prioritization of the portfolio's components.

The key outputs of the assess step activities are: the needs and goals for governance are clarified, the organization's change readiness is assessed, and the portfolio governance organizational structure and membership are defined. The key deliverable of the assess step is the portfolio governance charter.

- The portfolio governance charter may be a part of the portfolio charter or it may be a separate document. The portfolio governance charter authorizes and defines the governance organizational structure, membership, and roles. The charter describes the governance approach in order to meet organizational strategic and operational goals. The governance charter establishes clear, well-understood leadership agreements regarding the portfolio governance approach to oversee, contribute, support, or align the portfolio with organizational strategy. It also describes the degree of integration to existing organizational governance structures, policies, and procedures.

- The portfolio governance charter describes the linkage to existing organizational and portfolio governance and describes how governance will deliver value to the organization. When there is an existing portfolio governance charter, it should be updated to represent the enhanced governance.

- The portfolio governance charter is the key input to the plan step in order to create the portfolio governance management plan.

A1.1.2 Plan

The purpose of the plan step is to establish the governance organizational structure, roles, responsibilities, and authorities; governance-related processes; and required interactions. The outcome of this step is a portfolio governance management plan that details the portfolio's governance approach. The portfolio governance charter should be used as an input to the planning activities for purposes of creating the portfolio governance management plan. Based on the assessment results regarding organizational readiness, the portfolio governance management plan should address the culture by identifying key stakeholders who can influence change in the organization.

The planning activities will help to create the portfolio governance management plan, which should define the approach that will be taken to put in place the portfolio governance framework, processes, and organizational structure. The portfolio governance management plan describes the approach and intent of how governance will be managed, and it should include subsidiary plans for risk, performance, and communications management. The portfolio governance management plan may be a part of the portfolio management plan or it may be a separate document. The portfolio governance management plan should address any change management required to fully implement the portfolio governance functions and processes. Changes required to the existing governance organizational structure may require functional changes; resource reallocations; and new/revised roles, responsibilities, and authorities. The portfolio governance management plan activities are:

- **Plan governance approach and requirements.** Determine the approach for guidance and oversight of the portfolio and the individual portfolio components to enable the delivery of the portfolio's expected value and benefits.

- **Establish governance roles, responsibilities, and authorities.** Identify the governing body roles and responsibilities and the authority levels for decision-making areas. In addition, identify any other governance roles and responsibilities, including the portfolio managers; portfolio, program, or project management offices; program managers; project managers; and sponsors.

- **Establish governance processes.** Determine the governance approach, the resource needs, and the timeline required to develop and validate the creation or enhancement of governance processes. Refer to Section 3.5 and Table 3-1 for a description of portfolio governance domains, functions, and processes.

  o *Perform stakeholder analysis.* Perform stakeholder analysis of all areas that will be impacted by the governance framework, functions, and process changes. This will provide insight on influencers as well as barriers to the change.

  o *Perform resource assessment.* Identify governance resource capability and capacity needs for the team and determine whether in-house resources can be leveraged or additional resources will be needed.

  o *Determine performance measurements.* Define governance key performance indicators for the governing body to facilitate analysis and process improvements going forward.

  o *Define training and communications.* Establish the organizational change management approach, when applicable. Define the structured approach for transitioning individuals and groups to the governance processes. *Managing Change in Organizations: A Practice Guide* provides a detailed list of change management models and general guidelines. Develop a communications management plan that will include the types of information to be distributed to the organization regarding governance changes, timing, and training information.

The portfolio governance management plan includes the functions of oversight, control, integration, and decision making. When a current portfolio governance management plan exists, it may be updated for enhanced governance. Descriptions of the governance organizational structure, goals, roles, responsibilities, policies, procedures, and logistics for executing the governance functions and processes are summarized in the portfolio governance management plan. There may be separate, detailed documents for policies, procedures, and processes. The portfolio governance management plan should include but not be limited to the following:

- **Portfolio governance approach and requirements.** The portfolio governance management plan should describe the governance approach and the governance interaction requirements at the portfolio and component levels.

- **Governing body organizational structure and membership.** This is a description of the governance organizational structure (body, boards, and steering committees), members, roles, responsibilities, and decision-making authorities.

- **Individual team members, roles, and responsibilities.** These are the key stakeholders who will participate in the portfolio's governance functions and processes. The decision-making accountabilities and authorities are described.

- **Governance functions and processes.** The portfolio governance management plan should describe the governance functions and processes for the portfolio and components, and how they will be implemented. The portfolio governance management plan may provide for periodic reassessments to measure progress and detect adjustments required.

- **Benefits, performance metrics, and measurement.** The methods and metrics to evaluate the portfolio value and components benefits delivery should be identified as well as how they will be collected, consolidated, and reported. Examples include a balanced scorecard or dashboard.

- **Assumptions, constraints, and dependencies.** List assumptions; resource, budget, or operational constraints; and any dependencies on other areas that are part of the implementation.

- **Risk/issue escalation and reporting.** Describe the risk/issue escalation and reporting processes and standards.

- **Communication and training.** This is a description of how the governance functions and processes will be communicated. Communication and training should include the new governing body, the individuals stepping into new or modified roles, and the sponsor and stakeholders who are supporting the plan.

- **Reviews, health checks, and quality audits.** The requirements for portfolio component reviews and audits should be defined in the management plan and include scheduling, quality audits, and phase-gate reviews. A phase-gate review should include established governance functions and processes as well as determine whether a component is delivering results and benefits as planned.

- **Component initiation, closure, or transition.** The plan will outline the criteria and governance process for initiating, closing, or transitioning portfolio components. Governance approval to initiate components is typically based on a component business case. The plan should specify the criteria and process for closing or transitioning components.

 ©2016 Project Management Institute. *Governance of Portfolios, Programs, and Projects: A Practice Guide*

The approved portfolio governance management plan should be communicated to all stakeholders, especially to those required to achieve expected portfolio value and component results and benefits. The portfolio governance management plan is the key input to the implement step.

A1.1.3 Implement

The purpose of the implement step is to operationalize governance functions and processes, ensure effective organizational change, complete various governance reviews, and measure portfolio performance. The implement step activities include delivering governance functions and processes, managing organizational change, and monitoring and measuring governance performance. The implement step activities are:

- **Deliver governance functions and processes.** Document the functions and processes. This may include policies, procedures, tools, and techniques. A formal organizational policy may indicate which processes and tools need to be followed by the portfolio and components.

- **Manage organizational change.** Execute organizational change management based on the program governance plan or separate organizational change management plan.

  ○ *Deliver training and communications.* Communicate and train stakeholders based on needs. This should occur before the governance processes and reporting are operationalized and prior to component initiation. Report and track attendance, feedback, and results for potential required changes. Based on the complexity and risk of change, processes may be piloted and required updates made prior to broader implementation.

  ○ *Provide support services.* Provide organizational change management support during and immediately after implementation of governance processes and tools. Provide details on the mechanisms to request and receive support.

- **Monitor/measure governance performance.** Once the processes have been implemented, then begin to collect performance data and report as (a) performance of the processes, (b) level of adoption of the changes, and (c) results based on the performance parameters identified in the portfolio governance management plan. Adjust the plan to address any discrepancies.

  ○ *Review, authorize, and transition components.* Individual business cases for each component are reviewed and approved prior to component authorization based on the criteria outlined in the governance management plan.

  ○ *Perform audit reviews.* Reviews to assess the portfolio's progress are maintained separately from the component reviews.

  ○ *Monitor and measure benefits delivery.* The portfolio governance team monitors and measures the portfolio and portfolio components.

At the completion of the implement step, governance functions and processes have been operationalized, organizational change managed and supported, and portfolio governance performance reported. These are the key inputs to the improve step.

A1.1.4 Improve

The purpose of the improve step is to assess governance performance and identify improvement opportunities. Improve step activities are: (1) determine the performance and impact of governance processes, and (2) perform benefits sustainment. Governance processes should be evaluated for future improvement opportunities that the organization may leverage to enhance the effectiveness of governance.

Continuous improvement provides the ability for an organization to adjust governance processes based on performance measurements or changing conditions. Continuous improvement requires a structured change management approach. Change management is inherent in PMI's foundational standards including this practice guide. The portfolio governance framework implementation approach incorporates a continuous improvement life cycle by repeating the four steps of assess, plan, implement, and improve for enhancements to improve governance effectiveness. The improve step activities are:

- **Identify governance improvements.** Identify by performing the following activities:
  - *Review portfolio reports.* Portfolio reports may be a source of potential process improvements. Lessons learned at the component level may also be a source of improvements for governance when they are referenced by the organization for future portfolio enhancements. Lessons learned and good governance practices may be leveraged for future portfolio components, including programs and projects.
  - *Conduct impact analysis of governance processes.* When measurements are collected and reviewed after the implementation of any new or modified governance processes, the adoption should be evaluated based on the measurement methods identified in the portfolio governance management plan. A governance scorecard or dashboard can be used to communicate the performance measures and progress to achieve the targeted goals.

- **Perform benefits sustainment.** Governance ensures that the benefits provided by the organization's investment and efforts are sustained after component closure. There may be costs and a separate budget involved in overseeing ongoing benefits after component transition. The activities and costs required to sustain the benefits may be part of the portfolio or operations. An operational area may provide benefits sustainment activities.

The key output of this step is the governance improvement opportunities.

A1.2 Program Governance Framework Implementation Steps

The program governance framework implementation steps are provided in Sections A1.2.1 through A1.1.4 (see also Figure A1-2).

A1.2.1 Assess

The need for a program may be determined by the organization or the portfolio management team. Regardless of how the program is initiated, the purpose of the assess step is to develop a governance charter that is approved

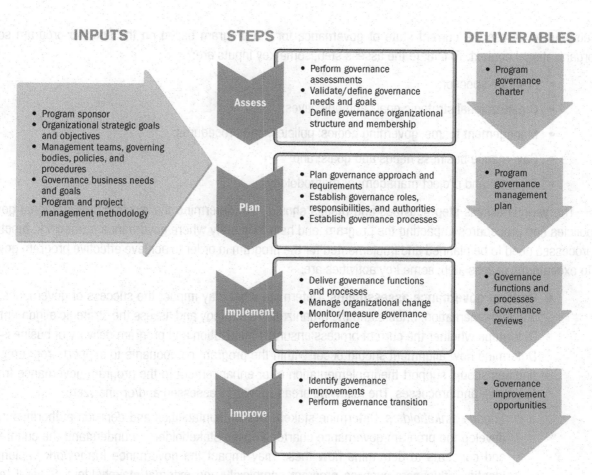

Figure A1-2. Program Governance Framework Implementation Steps

by a governing body. It is important to assess the current organizational, portfolio, and program governance that exists for a given program; therefore, the first step is to assess the current governance applicable to the program; determine the governance needs and goals for the program; and define the program's governance organizational structure and membership. In the absence of or immaturity of governance practices, the program manager and sponsor(s) should define and establish governance for the program.

Performing assessments and analyses assists the program manager and sponsor(s) in determining the current state of program governance along with the related functions and processes applicable to the program. The various assessment areas and risk analyses enable a gap analysis that bridges the current state with the program's planned governance. The assessment and gap analysis help to facilitate the development of a program governance charter that provides a recommended governance organizational structure and membership. The governance charter may be part of the program charter or may be a separate document.

The assessment activities and later steps of plan, implement, and improve activities should be owned and led by the program sponsor(s), program manager(s), and the established governing body. There may be several inputs required to assess the current state of governance for the program based on the specific program scope and organizational context. To initiate the assess step, some key inputs are:

- Program sponsor;
- Organizational strategic goals and objectives;
- Management teams, governing bodies, policies, and procedures;
- Governance business needs and goals; and
- Program and project management methodology.

The various assess step activities and results should help determine the existing organizational governance policies and procedures impacting the program, and help to identify where governance framework, functions, and processes need to be planned and implemented for the program in order to achieve effective program governance. To execute the assess step, some key activities are:

- **Perform governance assessments.** Determine what may impact the success of governance planning and implementation. Understand the organization's strategy and assess the strategic alignment process. Determine whether the current process ensures optimization and program delivery of business benefits. Determine how alignment should occur within the program components to support program goals. The findings should support the implementation of or enhancement to the program governance framework, functions, and processes. The following areas should be assessed and/or analyzed:

  o *Engage stakeholders.* Determine stakeholder accountabilities and decision authorities in order to develop the program governance charter. Engage stakeholders to understand the culture, politics, and concerns to determine how these may impact the governance framework implementation. Identify influencers such as program complexity and external stakeholders. Several techniques may be used to gather information such as surveys and open-ended questions during interviews or work sessions.

  o *Determine organizational processes and practices.* Assess the current governance organizational structure, policies, and procedures. Analyze the organizational governance oversight and decision-making support. Determine whether planning, control, delivery, transition, and benefits realization across program components will meet the intended benefits and, if not, determine the issues and causes. Determine the existing roles and responsibilities for oversight and decision making. Determine how strategic alignment and benefits realization will be monitored.

  o *Determine organizational capabilities and support.* Determine the organization's capabilities to support governance functions such as control, oversight, decision making, and integration. Areas to evaluate include PMOs, information systems, knowledge management, audit support, education, and training.

  o *Determine governance scope, goals, and success measures.* The desired future state for the program's governance should include which governance functions and processes are in and out of scope for the program, the governance goals, and objectives as well as the success measures.

Identify the governing body; identify new governance functions/processes or processes to be improved, such as strategic alignment and benefits identification and delivery; and include success metrics or results expected. Identify the business need and the value to be delivered. Link the need and value to the mission, vision, strategy, and goals of the organization.

- o *Perform gap analysis.* After completion of the governance current state assessment and desired future state, perform a gap analysis. The various assessment results that were performed should enable a gap analysis between the current state and the desired future state. When applicable to the program, describe the gaps between the current state and desired future state with justification for the change and the expected benefits.

- o *Perform SWOT/risk analyses.* Risks may be determined during the various analyses and after the identified desired future state and gap analysis. Analyze the strengths, weaknesses, opportunities, and threats to strategic alignment and benefits realization. Determine the impacts of risks identified to the attainment of program goals and business benefits. Determine how the rollout of the program's governance-related functions and processes will improve strategic alignment, integration management, and benefits realization.

- **Validate/define program governance needs and goals.** Based on the governance assessments, validate/define program governance needs and goals. Governance needs and goals are unique to an organization. The program business case and key stakeholders may provide direction for governance needs, goals, organizational structure, membership, and authorities. Examples of governance needs and goals are decision-making transparency, accountability, risk management, and a variety of others. The program governance plan should describe the governance goals and various decision criteria and authorities in areas such as phase-gate reviews, component initiation and transition, and resolution of escalated issues and risks.

- **Define governance organizational structure and membership.** The needs of the organization and the program's requirements form the basis for the governance structure. Based on various assessments and SWOT and/or risk analyses, define the program's required governance organizational structure and membership. The structure and members may be different for the program's governance versus the subprograms' and components' governance. Document in detail the structure, members, and roles including how the structure and membership will change during program benefits delivery as components are planned and authorized.

The key result or deliverable from the assess step activities is the approved program governance charter. The need and organizational structure for governance are clarified, the organization's change readiness is assessed, and the program governance organizational structure and membership are defined. The key deliverable of the assess step is the program governance charter. The governance charter may be part of the program charter or may be a separate charter. The program governance charter authorizes and defines the governance organizational structure, membership, and roles. The charter describes the governance approach in order to meet organizational strategic and operational goals. The governance charter establishes clear, well-understood leadership agreements as to the program governance approach to oversee, contribute, support, or align the program with organizational strategy;

conversely, the degree of autonomy for each will be given. It also describes the degree of integration with existing governance organizational structures, policies, and procedures. Chartering governance describes the linkage to any existing organizational governance and describes how governance will deliver value to the organization.

The approved program governance charter is the key input to the plan step.

A1.2.2 Plan

The purpose of the plan step is governance preparation in order to establish the governance organizational structure, roles, responsibilities, and authorities; governance-related processes; and required interactions. The outcome of this step is a program governance management plan that defines the program's governance approach in detail. When planning for change, people and cultural issues should be taken into consideration. Therefore, stakeholder involvement should be planned to include the approach, transition, and integration of governance functions and processes. Based on the program's extent of governance changes, the program governance management plan should balance organizational culture and change readiness with the implementation approach.

Planning activities will facilitate the development of a program governance management plan. Components of a program governance management plan are described in Section 6.2.4 of *The Standard for Program Management – Third Edition*. The program governance management plan may be a component of the program management plan or may be a separate plan.

The various planning activities include defining, documenting, and establishing the overall program and component governance approach; detailed roles, responsibilities, and authorities; decision making; and other processes in order to achieve effective program governance. Team resources should be identified and assigned, and working sessions should be facilitated with key stakeholders for planning activities based on the scope of governance to be implemented or enhanced. Some key activities to execute the plan step are:

- **Plan governance approach and requirements.** Determine the approach for guidance and oversight of the program as well as the individual components to enable the delivery of the program's goals and benefits.

- **Establish governance roles, responsibilities, and authorities.** Refer to Section 4.4 for a description of roles and responsibilities. Identify the roles, responsibilities, and decision-making authorities of the governing body, sponsor(s), program manager(s), project managers, key stakeholders, and PMO(s).

- **Establish governance processes.** Refer to Section 4.5 and Table 4-1 for a description of program governance domains, functions, and processes (e.g., decision making, risk escalation, change request, and various program-level and component review processes). The planning activities should focus on and identify how the targeted program governance processes will be created and implemented. Determine the resources, implementation approach, and timing to implement processes.

  - *Define training and communications.* Establish the organizational change management approach, when applicable. Define the structured approach for transitioning individuals and groups to the governance processes. *Managing Change in Organizations: A Practice Guide* provides a detailed list of change management models and general guidelines.

○ *Identify quality policies and communications.* The quality standards and policies should be identified for the program and applied across the program's components. Some examples of standards may be management processes, business validation of outputs, customer acceptance, testing parameters, or others based on industry and functional area.

The key results or deliverables from the planning activities are the approved governance management plan and subsidiary governance plans for risk, performance, and communications. The key deliverable of the plan step is:

- **Program governance management plan.** Descriptions of the governance organizational structure, goals, roles, responsibilities, policies, procedures, and logistics for executing the governance domains, functions, and processes are summarized in the program governance management plan. There may be separate, detailed documents for policies, procedures, and processes. The program governance management plan should include but not be limited to the following:

  ○ *Program governance approach and requirements.* Describe the governance approach and the governance interaction requirements at the program level and component level.

  ○ *Governing body structure and membership.* Describe the governance organizational structure (body, boards, and steering committees), members, roles, responsibilities, and decision-making authorities.

  ○ *Dependencies, assumptions, and constraints.* List governance key dependencies, assumptions, and constraints including resource, budget, and operational limitations.

  ○ *Individual team members, roles, and responsibilities.* Identify the key stakeholders who will participate in the program's governance functions and processes. Describe the decision-making accountabilities and authorities.

  ○ *Benefits, performance metrics, and measurement.* List the methods and metrics used to evaluate the program, identify components benefits delivery, and describe how the components will be collected, consolidated, and reported (e.g., a balanced scorecard or dashboard).

  ○ *Governance functions and processes.* Describe the governance functions and processes for the program and components and how they will be implemented. The plan may provide for periodic reassessments to measure progress and detect any required adjustments.

  ○ *Risk/issue escalation and reporting.* Describe the risk/issue escalation and reporting processes and standards.

  ○ *Communications and training.* Describe the communications and training during the program life cycle and the design, implementation, and support of the governance processes.

  ○ *Reviews, health checks, and quality audits.* Define the requirements for program and/or component reviews and audits, and include scheduling, conducting meetings, activities, quality audits, and phase-gate reviews. Describe the program-level phase-gate reviews. A program phase-gate review should include established governance functions and processes as well as whether a program is delivering benefits as planned.

- o *Component initiation, closure, or transition.* Outline the criteria and governance process for initiating, closing, or transitioning program components. Governance approval to initiate components is typically based on a component business case. Specify the criteria and process for closing or transitioning components.

- o *Support services.* Identify the areas where governance-related support is needed. Also describe the feedback and support approach used during the program.

- o *Stakeholder engagement.* List the stakeholders who should be engaged and communicated with during the program's life cycle and governance activities.

The approved program governance management plan should be communicated to all stakeholders, especially those who are required to be involved so as to achieve planned benefits and a successful program. Updates to the program governance management plan may be required based on changes to the organizational strategy; program strategy and plan; governing body's membership, responsibilities, and authorities; and governance policies, procedures, and process changes throughout the program's life cycle. The program governance management plan is the key input to the implement step.

A1.2.3 Implement

The purpose of the implement step is to operationalize governance functions and processes, manage organizational change, complete various governance reviews, and measure governance performance. The implement step activities include engaging stakeholders; executing functions and processes; reviewing, authorizing, and closing components; performing various reviews and audits; and monitoring and measuring governance performance.

During this step in the life cycle benefits delivery phase, as components are authorized, strategic alignment is reviewed and component business cases approved. Benefits delivery and compliance with reporting and control processes are monitored. The implement and improve step activities may be repeatable as components are completed and transitioned to operational areas. The key outcomes of the implement step are the operationalized governance functions and processes, managed organizational change, completed governance reviews, and measured governance performance. To execute the implement step, some key activities are:

- **Deliver governance functions and processes.** Document the governance functions and processes, which may include policies, procedures, tools, and techniques. A formal organizational policy may indicate which processes and tools are required by the program and the program's components.

- **Manage organizational change.** Execute organizational change management based on the program governance management plan or separate organizational change management plan.

  - o *Deliver training and communications.* Communicate and train stakeholders based on needs before the governance processes and reporting are operationalized and prior to component initiation. Report and track the attendance, feedback, and results for potential required changes. Based on the complexity and risk of change, processes may be piloted; therefore, make required updates prior to a broader implementation.

○ *Provide support services.* Provide organizational change management support during and immediately after implementation of governance processes and tools. Provide details on the means to request and receive support.

- **Monitor/measure governance performance.** Monitor and measure the governance performance in the following areas:

   ○ *Review, authorize, and transition components.* Review and approve individual business cases for each component prior to component authorization based on the criteria outlined in the governance management plan.

   ○ *Perform phase, performance, and audit reviews.* Reviews to assess the program's progress are maintained separately from the component reviews.

   ○ *Monitor and measure benefits delivery.* The program governance team monitors and measures the program and program components.

At the close of the implement step, governance functions and processes have been operationalized, governance reviews performed, and governance performance measured. These are key inputs to the improve step.

A1.2.4 Improve

The improve step is the fourth and final step in order to identify governance improvements and perform governance transition activities. The improve step also includes performing financial closure, program transition, program closure, and benefits sustainment. The improve step activities are:

- **Identify governance improvements.** Evaluate governance processes for future improvement opportunities that the organization may leverage to enhance the effectiveness of governance. Program reports may be a source of potential process improvements. Lessons learned at the program level may also be a source of improvements for governance that are referenced by the organization for future programs. Lessons learned and good governance practices may be leveraged for future programs, particularly during the program definition phase for governance risk, performance, and communication planning.

- **Perform governance transition.** Governance activities may include program governance and knowledge transition activities.

   ○ *Perform program closure.* Conduct a final program phase-gate review prior to approval of the program closure. The governing body approves the recommendation for program closure. The business case, program governance management plan, and stakeholder engagement plan should specify the minimal acceptance criteria and measures for the program; stakeholder satisfaction of performance should be reviewed and the performance assessed. Once closure is approved and benefits sustainment is started, the program closure begins. Program budgets are closed and communicated to stakeholders. Closure information is in the closing statements and summarized in the final program performance report. During the program closure phase, the governance transition is planned and the ongoing responsibility is transferred. The governing body determines whether all of the planned consolidated benefits have been met or will be met upon program transition.

○ *Perform benefits sustainment.* Governance ensures that benefits provided by the organization's investment and efforts are sustained after program closure. There may be activities to transition the program governance to another entity in order to monitor and oversee ongoing benefits. There may be costs and a separate budget involved in overseeing ongoing benefits after program transition. The activities and costs required to sustain the benefits may be part of a portfolio, program, project, or operations. An operational area may provide benefits sustainment activities.

The key output of this step is the improvement opportunities supported by final closure reports. Closure reports may be related to governance, performance, finances, risk, or benefits. Information in these reports may provide improvement opportunities for future program governance.

A1.3 Project Governance Framework Implementation Steps

The project governance framework implementation steps are provided in Sections A1.3.1 through A1.3.4 (see Figure A1-3).

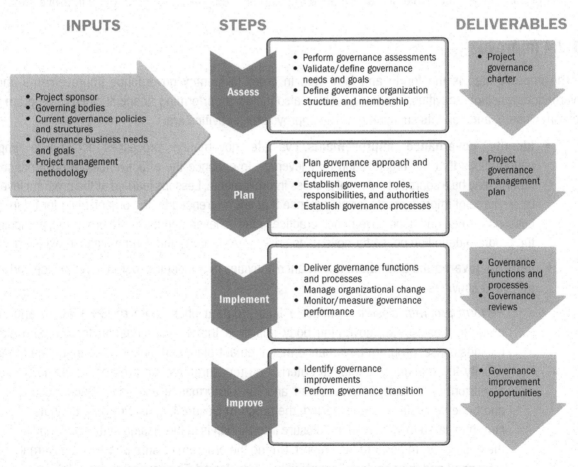

Figure A1-3. Project Governance Framework Implementation Steps

A1.3.1 Assess

The purpose of the assess step is to develop a governance charter that is approved by a governing body. The governance charter may be a part of the project charter or may be a separate charter. Assessment of the organizational environment and the current project governance needs and requirements are required to facilitate the development of a project governance charter. Before planning and implementing project governance, it is crucial to assess the organization's current state of project governance and related functions and processes. This assessment enables a gap analysis of the current state and the desired future state, which will assist the project manager and sponsor(s) in determining related functions and processes applicable to the project. Since the implementation is based upon this assessment, which is unique for each project, the framework can be tailored to the organization's environment.

These assessment activities and later steps of plan, implement, and improve should be owned and led by the project sponsor(s), project manager(s), and the established governing body. There may be several inputs required to assess the current state of governance for the project based on the specific project scope and organizational context. To initiate the assess step, the key inputs are:

- Project sponsor,
- Governing bodies,
- Current governance policies and structures,
- Governance business needs and goals, and
- Project management methodology.

The various assessment activities and results should determine the existing governance policies and procedures impacting the project and where governance framework, functions, and processes need to be planned and implemented for the project in order to achieve effective project governance.

The assess step activities are as follows:

- **Perform governance assessments.** Areas that may be assessed are current governance structure, policies, standards, and processes, as well as project management methodologies, support, guidance, and lessons learned.

- **Gather information.** Several techniques and analyses may be used to gather information such as SWOT and risk analyses, surveys, and open-ended questions during interviews or work sessions. By using SWOT and risk analyses, analyze the organization's strengths, weaknesses, opportunities, threats, gaps, and risks to strategic alignment and the delivery of products, services, and results to better assist the organization when implementing project governance. Determine the impacts of risks identified on the attainment of project goals and objectives. Determine how the rollout of governance-related functions and processes would improve the delivery of products, services, and results.

- **Determine organization's capabilities.** Determine the organization's capabilities to support governance functions such as oversight, decision making, control, and integration. Analyze the current guidelines and constraints that may limit the implementation of project governance. Areas to evaluate include the project management office, information systems, knowledge management, audit support, education, and training. The organization's current resources, capacity, or capability should be taken into account in determining the approach to project governance implementation or improvement.

- **Perform stakeholder analysis.** Perform a stakeholder analysis to provide insight on possible barriers that may impact the ability to execute a successful project. Understanding the barriers helps to determine which methods to use to influence the stakeholders. Engage stakeholders to understand the culture, politics, and concerns and to determine how these may impact the management and delivery of the product, service, or result. Identify influencers such as project or organizational complexity, politics, culture, and external stakeholders. Several techniques may be used to gather information such as surveys and open-ended questions during interviews or work sessions.

- **Validate/define governance needs and goals.** Governance needs and goals are unique to an organization. The project scope and key stakeholders may provide direction for governance needs, goals, organizational structure, membership, and authorities. Examples of governance needs and goals are decision-making transparency, accountability, risk management, and a variety of others.

- **Define project governance organizational structure and membership.** The structure is defined based on the needs of the organization and the project's requirements. Define the project's required governance structure based on stakeholder analysis, various assessments, and SWOT or risk analyses. Document in detail the structure, members, roles, and responsibilities.

The key deliverable or output of the assess step is the project governance charter.

The project governance charter is approved by the governing body and authorizes the formation of the project governance framework. The charter describes how the project will be governed in order to meet organizational strategic and project goals; establishes clear, well-understood leadership agreements as to how project governance will oversee, contribute, support, or align the project with organizational strategy; and, conversely, establishes the degree of autonomy that each will be given. The project governance charter also describes the degree of integration with existing organizational governance structures, policies, and procedures; explains the linkage to any existing organizational governance; and describes how governance will deliver value to the organization. The project governance charter is the key input to the plan step in order to create the governance management plan.

A1.3.2 Plan

The purpose of the plan step is to prepare to establish the governance organizational structure, roles, responsibilities, and authorities; governance-related processes; and required interactions. The output of this step is a project governance management plan that details the project's governance approach. The plan should consider how to manage organizational change as governance is implemented. Therefore, stakeholder involvement should be planned to include the approach, transition, and integration of governance changes. Based on the extent of governance changes, the governance management plan should balance organizational culture and change readiness with the implementation approach.

Charter and planning activities will facilitate the development of a project governance management plan. This plan should define roles and responsibilities and establish a decision-making structure. The plan step activities are:

- **Plan governance approach and requirements.** Determine the approach and requirements for governance guidance and oversight of the project based on the assessment results. Determine the governance-supporting processes and activities required to enable the successful delivery of the project's unique product, service, or result.

- **Establish governance roles, responsibilities, and authorities.** Refer to Section 5.4 for a description of the roles and responsibilities. Identify the governing body roles, responsibilities, and decision-making authorities and those of the project management office, project manager, and sponsor(s).

- **Establish governance processes.** Refer to Section 5.5 and Table 5-1 for a description of project governance domains, functions, and processes. The planning activities should focus on and identify how the targeted project governance processes will be created and implemented. Determine the resources, implementation approach, and timing to implement processes.

The key result or deliverable from the planning activities is the approved project governance management plan. The key deliverable of the plan step is:

- **Project governance management plan.** The project governance management plan describes the governance structure, goals, roles, responsibilities, policies, procedures, and logistics for executing the governance functions and processes. There may be separate, detailed documents for policies, procedures, and processes. The project governance management plan should include but not be limited to the following:

  - *Goals and objectives.* The project governance management plan should align with the charter's objectives and scope. The plan should describe the governance approach and the governance interaction requirements at the project level.

  - *Governing body structure and membership.* This is a description of the governance structure (body, boards, and steering committees), members, roles, responsibilities, and decision-making authorities.

  - *Individual team members, roles, and responsibilities.* These are the key stakeholders who will participate in the project's governance functions and processes. The decision-making accountabilities and authorities are described.

  - *Stakeholder engagement.* List the stakeholders to be engaged and communicated with during the project's life cycle and governance activities.

  - *Project governance functions and processes.* The project governance management plan should describe the governance functions and processes for the project and how they will be implemented.

The plan may provide for periodic reassessments to measure progress and detect adjustments that may be required.

○ *Communications and training.* This should describe the communications and training during the project life cycle and support of the governance processes.

○ *Support services.* The areas where governance-related support is needed should be identified. The feedback and support approach during the project should be described.

To ensure a successful implementation, the approved project governance management plan should be communicated to all stakeholders, especially those who are required to be involved. The project governance management plan is the key input to the implement step.

A1.3.3 Implement

The purpose of the implement step is to operationalize governance functions and processes, manage organizational change, complete various governance reviews, and measure project governance performance. The implement step activities include engaging stakeholders, executing functions and processes, performing various reviews and audits, and monitoring and measuring project governance performance. The outcomes of this step are the established governing body, implemented functions and processes, completed communications, project performance reports, and governance reviews. Engaging stakeholders is critical when preparing the organization for change and making decisions. The implement step activities are:

- **Deliver governance functions and processes.** Document the functions and processes. This may include policies, procedures, tools, and techniques. Establish the governance structure, members, roles, responsibilities, and decision-making authorities.

- **Manage organizational change.** Execute organizational change management based on the project governance management plan or a separate organizational change management plan.

- **Monitor and measure performance.** Monitor and measure the project's progress based on the project governance management plan. Update the project governance management plan, as applicable, to address the required changes and updates. Perform governance reviews and audits to assess the progress of the project within the stated conditions and parameters.

At the close of the implement step, governance functions and processes have been operationalized, reviews performed, and progress reported. These are key inputs to the improve step.

A1.3.4 Improve

The improve step is the fourth and final step in order to identify governance improvements and perform governance transition activities. The improve step also includes performing project closure and benefits sustainment. The outcomes of this step are the performance assessment, improvement opportunities, and closure report. Information in these reports may provide improvement opportunities for project governance in the future. The improve step activities are:

- **Identify governance improvements.** Obtaining feedback from stakeholders and documenting the lessons learned enable the governing body and sponsoring organization to consider future improvement opportunities.

- **Perform governance transition.** Transition activities may include project governance and knowledge transition activities.

  - *Perform project closure.* There should be a final project phase-gate review prior to approval of final closure of the project. The governing body approves the recommendation for project closure. The business case and project governance management plan, including the stakeholder engagement plan, should specify the minimal acceptance criteria and measures for the project; therefore, stakeholder satisfaction of performance should be reviewed and the performance assessed. Once the governing body approves project closure, project budgets are closed and communicated to stakeholders. Closure information is placed in the closing statements and summarized in the final project performance report.

  - *Perform benefits sustainment.* Governance ensures that benefits provided by the organization's investment and efforts are sustained after project closure. There may be activities to transition the project governance to another entity in order to monitor and oversee ongoing benefits. There may be costs and a separate budget involved in overseeing ongoing benefits after project transition. An operational area may provide benefits sustainment activities.

At the completion of the improve step, the performance assessment, identification of improvement opportunities, and closure reports are completed. Information in these reports may provide opportunities to improve project governance in the future.

APPENDIX X1
CONTRIBUTORS AND REVIEWERS OF *GOVERNANCE OF PORTFOLIOS, PROGRAMS, AND PROJECTS: A PRACTICE GUIDE*

This appendix lists, alphabetically within groupings, those individuals and organizations that have contributed to the development and production of *Governance of Portfolios, Programs, and Projects: A Practice Guide.*

The Project Management Institute is grateful to all of these individuals for their support and acknowledges their contributions to the project management profession.

X1.1 Core Committee Members

The following individuals served as members, were contributors of text or concepts, and served as leaders within the Project Core Committee:

Guillermo Blanco Hernández, PMP
Mustafa Hafizoglu, MSc, PMP
Mark T.W. Lam, MSc, PMP
Francesca Pratt, MBA, PMP
Jen L. Skrabak, PfMP, PMP, Chair
Gwen Whitman, EMBA, PfMP, Vice Chair
Lorna Scheel, MSc, PMI Standards Compliance Specialist

X1.2 Subject Matter Experts Reviewers

In addition to the members of the committee, the following individuals provided their review and recommendations on drafts of the standard:

Angie Bates, MBA, PfMP
Joyce D. Brown, PMP, CBAP
Thomas Carlqvist, MSc, PMP
Colette J. Connor, PMP
Darya Duma, PEng, PMP
Wayne D. Ellis, PE, PMP
Iain Fraser, Dip PPC, PMP, PMI Fellow
Richard J. Heaslip, PhD
Lucia Italiano, PMP

Walther Krause, PMP
Ginger Levin, PhD, PgMP, PMP
Warren R. Long, P. Eng, PMP
Jianfeng Ma, PMP, MSP Advanced Practitioner
Mercedes Martinez Sanz, PMP
Oyinkansola A. Ogundalu, PMP, CBAP
Laureen Pfizenmaier, PMP
Hamidur Rahman Adnan, PfMP, PgMP
Palani Vel Rajan, PMP
Michael Reed, PfMP, PMP
Ivan D. Rincon, CISA, PMP
Gary Scherling, PMP, PMOC
Fernando Schmidkonz, MBA, PMP
Rommert Stellingwerf, MSc, PMP
Edward W. Sullivan, PMP
Galen Townson, EMBA, PMP
Angelo Valle
Michael A. Yinger

X1.3 Member Advisory Group (MAG) Review

The following individuals served as members of the PMI Standards Program Member Advisory Group and voted on the final draft of *Governance of Portfolios, Programs, and Projects: A Practice Guide:*

Laurence Goldsmith, MBA, PMP
Hagit Landman, MBA, PMP, PMI-SP
Yvan Petit, PhD, PfMP
Chris Stevens, PhD
Dave Violet, MPM, PMP
John Zlockie, MBA, PMP, PMI Standards Manager

X1.4 Production Staff

Special mention is due to the following employees of PMI:

Donn Greenberg, Manager, Publications
Roberta Storer, Product Editor
Barbara Walsh, Publications Production Supervisor

APPENDIX X2
SUMMARY OF RESEARCH FINDINGS CONCERNING THE GOVERNANCE OF PROJECTS, PROGRAMS, AND PORTFOLIOS

This appendix is an excerpt from an internal PMI research report from December 2014.

X2.1 Purpose

The specific goal of this report was to review the project management and allied disciplines research to seek evidence-based findings on project, program, and portfolio (PPP) governance that should be considered in the formulation of future standards. This study reviewed the relationship between published research on the effects of governance from a broad range of literature from 2000 to 2014 (1,500 abstracts read, 206 coded for inclusion in study).

X2.2 Findings

The findings suggest that the current standards reflect commonly held beliefs (and confusion) about project governance as reported in gray literature, blogs, and much PM literature, but does not reflect some existing evidence-based findings available in the research literature. This suggests there is room for research on governance to make a contribution to governance standards development.

The definitions of project, program, and portfolio governance in both research and standards suffer from: conflation of the concepts of management and governance; confusion between the governance needs of different levels of project, program, and portfolio management; and lack of a way to distinguish between the governance needs of the owner/sponsor, the project, the organizational network, and project-based organizations.

A particular contribution that PMI standards could make is the differentiation between the different levels and domains of project governance. Providing a consistent definition and understanding of the different types of governance inherent in project, program, and portfolio management would help both researchers and practitioners focus their efforts on the appropriate mechanisms. It could also help begin to develop additive, evidence-based research on governance.

Table X2-1 summarizes the findings around the questions investigated.

Table X2-1. Summary of Research Findings

Research Question Investigated	Findings Summary
1. How do research literature and standards define PPP governance? What are the definitions being used for PPP governance? What are the common components among these definitions?	Governance research in the allied disciplines draws from rich streams of governance research going back 50 years and appears to use definitions that contain elements of oversight and direction usually at the top levels of organizations. While there are several definitions in use, each is associated with a particular research stream, and researchers clearly delineate how what they are studying ties in with these streams. Recent work is beginning to extend governance as a need throughout organizations instead of just at the top.
	Governance research in project-related journals tends to use a wide assortment of definitions and trends and often conflates governance with management. There is confusion between governance of a single project, governance over a project, governance of project management, and governance of complex networks of organizations.
	PMI standards (as of 2014) provide several definitions in relation to different levels of project management operating in organizations. Given the recognized need to tailor governance to the organization it is being designed for, and thinking about projects, portfolios, and programs being managed at different levels of an organization, this approach may be justified. However, PMI standards continue the research trend of conflating management and governance activities.
	Other PPP standards bodies tend to use a corporate or high-level definition of governance as relating to the activities of senior executives and boards in developing direction and control systems. Most often, it is defined as those areas of corporate governance that are directly related to project activities.
2. What is the current state of research that has been conducted on PPP governance?	There is little to no empirical evidence apparent of PPP-specific governance outside of project-related journals except in IT journals. There is almost no empirical evidence of the effectiveness of PPP governance other than sponsorship and steering committees.
	There is a long-standing and growing body of empirical evidence that effective project sponsorship impacts both project management and project business success.
	There is a growing body of empirical literature exploring the role of the steering committee. Results are ambiguous.
	There is conflation of governance and management.
	Everyone in the project literature seems to assume they understand the term "governance" and either do not define what they mean by it or use their own definition rather than building on others, and specifically not building on the general management literature.
	There seems to be growing focus on governance and efforts to produce evidence as indicated by publications in 2014.
3. What does research reveal about the structural relationships between corporate governance and portfolio, program, and project governance?	There is very little empirical work.
	In most research, the structural relations are suggested to work as follows:
	• Corporate-level governance focuses on oversight and direction through the mechanism of portfolio management and the creation of OPM frameworks.
	• Sponsors, steering committees, and portfolio management bodies (of projects and programs) provide the linkage between project management and strategic management and corporate governance.
	• Project and program management are at the management level.
	Some empirical studies address the need for alignment between levels and the transfer of control modes between levels in the organization. IT studies present some empirical evidence in the IT governance context. By far, the most research into governance structures and project sponsors can be found in the IT literature.
	A recent study by Müller et al. (2014)[A] begins to provide foundations for this work.
	In the world of engineering and construction projects, governance issues are resolved through the nexus of contracts that form the rules by which the project is governed. There is a growing body of literature looking at the role of relational and formal contracting in governing these projects.
4. What does research reveal about the relationships among the project sponsor, the project steering committee, and portfolio, program, and project governance? How do these roles and structures interact? What challenges (if any) are associated with these structures working together? According to research, what are the optimal characteristics of effective governance that facilitate successful delivery of projects and programs?	There is solid evidence of the importance of the sponsor role, both as a support role in project management supporting the project manager in delivering the project as per the plan, and as a governance role monitoring and controlling the delivery of business benefits through project delivery.
	There is ambiguous evidence on steering committees; there is some empirical evidence supporting their benefit but confusion over whether the benefits come from a steering (decision-making) or advisory (stakeholder) committee. There is concern that the steering committee reduces the authority and decision-making power of the sponsor.
	There is little discussion of the relationships among the sponsor, steering committee, and portfolio, program, or project management except in rich case study examples that highlight how different these relations are across organizations.
	There is some discussion in both practical and PPP conceptual literature of how these relationships should work, but little in the way of empirical evidence.
	Müller et al. (2014) provide some foundation evidence that the Müller (2009)[B] depiction of four models of project governance appears to be common in practice. Future research needs to test the contingency factors that influence the choice of these models and whether any of them support more effective project delivery.
	There is a growing amount of research on the tradeoffs, costs, and challenges of implementing governance.

Research Question Investigated	Findings Summary
5. What research on effective governance is not reflected in PMI's foundational standards?	There is a difference between governance and management. Governance provides oversight and direction for management (making sure the right thing is done). Management is the implementation, monitoring, control, and direction for productive activities (making sure the work is done right).
	Effective governance involves the least amount of structure as possible because there are costs associated with governance structure and monitoring mechanisms and they often result in unintended consequences.
	People respond to the type of governance imposed. Rigid, formal governance structures drive out initiative, innovation, and trust.
	Müller's (2009) model crossing shareholder versus stakeholder orientation with outcome versus behavioral controls seems to be proving out in empirical research and is a model to watch for contextual factors that influence effective governance.
6. What PPP governance practices or mechanisms, evidenced by research, should be included in the four PMI foundational standards?	PMI standards should include more information on the available mechanisms for implementing governance at various levels of project management activity within organizations.
	Specifically, five types of governance mechanisms should be discussed in the appropriate PMI standards:
	• Impersonal governance, • Personal governance, • Vertical authority, • Informal, horizontal, or lateral relations, and • Formal governance.
	There is also a wider array of organizational governance structures that could be considered over and above the sponsor and steering committee that might prove useful. Standards need to provide much more information and guidance on how to select among the governance mechanisms because "good" governance is context dependent.
	PMI standards need to differentiate clearly between project management activities and governance activities.

[A]Müller, R., Pemsel, S., & Shao, J. (2014). Organizational enablers for governance and governmentality of projects: A literature review. *International Journal of Project Management, 32*(8), 1309–1320.

[B]Müller, R. (2009). *Project Governance (Fundamentals of Project Management).* Farnham, U.K.: Gower.

GLOSSARY

Ambiguity. A state of being unclear, of not knowing what to expect or how to comprehend a situation.

Assumption. A factor in the planning process that is considered to be true, real, or certain, without proof or demonstration.

Benefits Realization. The successful integration of the change into business as usual.

Business Impact Analysis. A technique used to evaluate the potential business consequences of a proposed change.

Business Value. A concept that is unique to each organization and includes tangible and intangible elements. Through the effective use of project, program, and portfolio management disciplines, organizations will possess the ability to employ reliable, established processes to meet enterprise objectives and obtain greater business value from their investments.

Change Management. A comprehensive, cyclic, and structured approach for transitioning individuals, groups, and organizations from a current state to a future state with intended business benefits.

Change Readiness Assessment. A measure of the reality of the current organization in relation to the future state from two perspectives: organizational systems and structures that need to be improved or will support the change; and the people and culture that are able to support or may resist the change.

Change Request. A formal proposal to modify any document, deliverable, or baseline.

Communications Management Plan. A component of the project, program, or portfolio management plan that describes how, when, and by whom information will be administered and disseminated. See also *governance management plan, portfolio management plan, program management plan,* and *project management plan.*

Complexity. A characteristic of a program or project or its environment which is difficult to manage due to human behavior, system behavior, and ambiguity.

Constraint. A limiting factor that affects the execution of a project, program, portfolio, or process.

Control Function. The processes and activities that provide monitoring, measuring, and reporting for portfolios, programs, and projects. See also *governance function, oversight function, integration function,* and *decision-making function.*

Critical Success Factor. The high-level objectives of the portfolio, program, or project and the contributing enablers that are required to be in place to ensure outcomes.

Culture. An explicit way of working (the formal systems and processes in place and how they operate) and a tacit level of operation (the informal and semiformal networks and other activities people employ to get things done and bypass, subvert, or seek to influence the more formal processes).

Decision-Making Function. The processes and activities that provide structure and delegations of authority for portfolios, programs, and projects. See also *governance function, control function, integration function,* and *oversight function.*

Deliverable. Any unique and verifiable product, result, or capability to perform a service that is produced to complete a process, phase, or project.

Enterprise Environmental Factors. Conditions, not under the immediate control of the team, that influence, constrain, or direct the project, program, or portfolio.

Functional Organization. An organizational structure in which staff is grouped by areas of specialization and the project manager has limited authority to assign work and apply resources.

Governance Alignment Domain. The governance domain of functions and processes to create and maintain an integrated governance framework. See also *governance domain, governance risk domain, governance performance domain,* and *governance communications domain.*

Governance Charter. A document that authorizes the formation of the governing body and the resources to implement or enhance governance framework, functions, and processes, and describes the linkage to existing organizational governance. See also *portfolio charter, program charter,* and *project charter.*

Governance Communications Domain. The governance domain of functions and processes to disseminate information, engage stakeholders, and ensure organizational change. See also *governance domain, governance alignment domain, governance risk domain,* and *governance performance domain.*

Governance Domain. A set of functions carried out by an individual, group, or organization to address a specific governance area of concentration. See also *governance alignment domain, governance risk domain, governance performance domain,* and *governance communications domain.*

Governance Framework. The totality of the four governance domains for portfolios, programs, and projects: governance alignment domain, governance risk domain, governance performance domain, and governance communications domain. See also *governance domain* and *governance function.*

Governance Function. A grouping of processes related to each other and across governance domains that are performed in order to support governance for portfolios, programs, and projects. See also *governance domain.*

Governance Gap Analysis. A technique used to determine gaps between the current state and the future state with the purpose of assessing strengths and weaknesses in the governance framework. See also *governance framework.*

Governance Management Plan. A document that describes the governance framework, functions, and processes that guide organizational project management, portfolio, program, or project management activities. See also *portfolio management plan, program management plan,* and *project management plan.*

Governance Performance Domain. The governance domain of functions and processes to ensure measurement and evaluation of key performance indicators (KPIs) against parameters and realization of business value. See also *governance domain, governance alignment domain, governance risk domain,* and *governance communications domain.*

Governance Risk Domain. The governance domain of functions and processes to identify and resolve threats and opportunities to ensure balance of risk and reward. See also *governance domain, governance alignment domain, governance performance domain,* and *governance communications domain.*

Governing Body. A temporary or permanent organized group consisting of members by areas of responsibility and authority to provide guidance and decision making for portfolios, programs, and projects.

Integration Function. The processes and activities that provide strategic alignment for portfolios, programs, and projects. See also *governance function, control function, oversight function,* and *decision-making function.*

Issue. A threat that has occurred. See also *opportunity, risk,* and *threat.*

Key Performance Indicators. A set of performance measures critical to the success of the endeavor.

Lessons Learned. The knowledge gained during a project which shows how project events were addressed or should be addressed in the future for the purpose of improving future performance.

Methodology. A system of practices, techniques, procedures, and rules used by those who work in a discipline.

Milestone. A significant point or event in a project, program, or portfolio.

Non-governmental organization. An organization that is not part of a government.

Opportunity. A risk that would have a positive effect on one or more project objectives. See also *issue, risk,* and *threat.*

Organization. The entity that may include all levels of an enterprise and may transcend business lines or divisions, including any areas/business units that have impact, influence, or involvement in project and business operations.

Organizational Environment. The policies and supporting practices of the organization that are created to support the organizational project management strategy execution framework and delivery of the organization's strategy.

Organizational Governance. The structured way to provide control, direction, and coordination through people, policies, and processes to meet organizational strategic and operational goals. See also *organizational project management (OPM) governance, portfolio governance, program governance,* and *project governance.*

Organizational Process Assets. Plans, processes, policies, procedures, and knowledge bases specific to and used by the performing organization.

Organizational Project Management. A framework in which portfolio, program, and project management are integrated with organizational enablers in order to achieve strategic objectives.

Organizational Project Management (OPM) Governance. The framework, functions, and processes that guide organizational project management activities in order to align portfolio, program, and project management practices to meet organizational strategic and operational goals. See also *organizational governance, portfolio governance, program governance,* and *project governance.*

Organizational Project Management Maturity. The level of an organization's ability to deliver the desired strategic outcomes in a predictable, controllable, and reliable manner.

Oversight Function. The processes and activities that provide guidance, direction, and leadership for portfolios, programs, and projects. See also *governance function, control function, decision-making function,* and *integration function.*

Performance Management Plan. A component of the project, program, or portfolio management plan that describes how performance management activities will be structured and performed. See also *portfolio management plan, program management plan,* and *project management plan.*

Phase Gate. A review at the end of a phase in which a decision is made to continue to the next phase, to continue with modification, or to end a project or program. See also *project phase.*

Portfolio. Projects, programs, subportfolios, and operations managed as a group to achieve strategic objectives. See also *program* and *project.*

Portfolio Balancing. The process of optimizing the mix of portfolio components to further the strategic objectives of the organization.

Portfolio Charter. A document issued by a sponsor that authorizes and specifies the portfolio structure and links the portfolio to the organization's strategic objectives. See also *governance charter, program charter,* and *project charter.*

Portfolio Governance. The framework, functions, and processes that guide portfolio management activities in order to optimize investments to meet organizational strategic and operational goals. See also *organizational governance, organizational project management (OPM) governance, program governance,* and *project governance.*

Portfolio Management. The centralized management of one or more portfolios to achieve strategic objectives. See also *program management* and *project management.*

Portfolio Management Office. A management structure that standardizes the portfolio-related governance processes and facilitates the sharing of resources, methodologies, tools, and techniques. See also *program management office* and *project management office.*

Portfolio Management Plan. A document that specifies how a portfolio will be organized, monitored, and controlled. See also *program management plan* and *project management plan.*

Portfolio Management Process Cycle. A series of iterative, continuous, and related processes that are integrated into ongoing organizational processes.

Portfolio Manager. The person or group assigned by the performing organization to establish, balance, monitor, and control portfolio components in order to achieve strategic business objectives. See also *program manager* and *project manager.*

Program. A group of related projects, subprograms, and program activities that are managed in a coordinated way to obtain benefits not available from managing them individually. See also *portfolio* and *project*.

Program Charter. A document issued by a sponsor that authorizes the program management team to use organizational resources to execute the program and links the program to the organization's strategic objectives. See also *governance charter, portfolio charter,* and *project charter.*

Program Governance. The framework, functions, and processes that guide program management activities in order to deliver business value to meet organizational strategic and operational goals. See also *organizational governance, organizational project management (OPM) governance, portfolio governance,* and *project governance.*

Program Life Cycle Management. Managing all program activities related to program definition, program benefits delivery, and program closure.

Program Management. The application of knowledge, skills, tools, and techniques to a program to meet the program requirements and to obtain benefits and control not available by managing projects individually. See also *portfolio management* and *project management.*

Program Management Office. A management structure that standardizes the program-related governance processes and facilitates the sharing of resources, methodologies, tools, and techniques. See also *portfolio management office* and *project management office.*

Program Management Plan. A document that integrates the program's subsidiary plans and establishes the management controls and overall plan for integrating and managing the program's individual components. See also *portfolio management plan* and *project management plan.*

Program Manager. The person authorized by the performing organization to lead the team or teams responsible for achieving program objectives. See also *portfolio manager* and *project manager.*

Project. A temporary endeavor undertaken to create a unique product, service, or result. See also *portfolio* and *program.*

Project Budget. The sum of work package cost estimates, contingency reserve, and management reserve.

Project Charter. A document issued by the project initiator or sponsor that formally authorizes the existence of a project and provides the project manager with the authority to apply organizational resources to project activities. See also *governance charter, portfolio charter,* and *program charter.*

Project Governance. The framework, functions, and processes that guide project management activities in order to create a unique product, service, or result to meet organizational strategic and operational goals. See also *organizational governance, organizational project management (OPM) governance,* and *portfolio governance.*

Project Life Cycle. The series of phases that a project passes through from its initiation to its closure.

Project Management. The application of knowledge, skills, tools, and techniques to project activities to meet the project requirements. See also *portfolio management* and *program management.*

Project Management Office. A management structure that standardizes the project-related governance processes and facilitates the sharing of resources, methodologies, tools, and techniques. See also *portfolio management office* and *program management office.*

Project Management Plan. The document that describes how the project will be executed, monitored and controlled, and closed. See also *governance management plan, portfolio management plan, program management plan, communications management plan, performance management plan,* and *risk management plan.*

Project Manager. The person assigned by the performing organization to lead the team that is responsible for achieving the project objectives. See also *portfolio manager* and *program manager.*

Project Phase. A collection of logically related project activities that culminates in the completion of one or more deliverables. See also *phase gate.*

Project Schedule. An output of a schedule model that presents linked activities with planned dates, durations, milestones, and resources.

RACI. A common type of responsibility assignment matrix that uses responsible, accountable, consult, and inform statuses to define the involvement of stakeholders in project activities.

Requirement. A condition or capability that is required to be present in a product, service, or result to satisfy a contract or other formally imposed specification.

Responsibility Assignment Matrix. A grid that shows the project resources assigned to each work package.

Risk. An uncertain event or condition that, if it occurs, has a positive or negative effect on one or more project objectives. See also *issue, opportunity,* and *threat.*

Risk Appetite. The degree of uncertainty an organization or individual is willing to accept in anticipation of a reward. See also *risk threshold* and *risk tolerance.*

Risk Management Plan. A component of the project, program, or portfolio management plan that describes how risk management activities will be structured and performed. See also *governance management plan, portfolio management plan, program management plan,* and *project management plan.*

Risk Mitigation. A risk response strategy whereby the project team acts to decrease the probability of occurrence or impact of a threat. See also *threat.*

Risk Threshold. The level of risk exposure above which risks are addressed and below which risks may be accepted. See also *risk appetite* and *risk tolerance.*

Risk Tolerance. The degree of uncertainty that an organization or individual is willing to withstand. See also *risk appetite* and *risk threshold.*

Roadmap. A portfolio or program document that provides the high-level strategic direction of the portfolio or program in a chronological fashion for depicting dependencies, major milestones, and decision points, and linking the business strategy and the portfolio or program work.

Sponsor. An individual or a group that provides resources and support for the project, program, or portfolio, and is accountable for enabling success. See also *stakeholder*.

Stakeholder. An individual, group, or organization that may affect, be affected by, or perceive itself to be affected by a decision, activity, or outcome of a project, program, or portfolio. See also *sponsor*.

Stakeholder Analysis. A technique of systematically gathering and analyzing quantitative and qualitative information to determine whose interests should be taken into account throughout the project.

SWOT Analysis. Analysis of strengths, weaknesses, opportunities, and threats of an organization, project, or option.

System. A collection of various components that together can produce results not attainable by the components alone.

Threat. A risk that would have a negative effect on one or more project objectives. See also *issue, opportunity,* and *risk*.

Uncertainty. A lack of understanding and awareness of issues, events, path to follow, or solutions to pursue. Uncertainty may increase and amplify issues, risks, behaviors, or situations which are internal and external to a program or project.

INDEX

in project governance, 73
Stakeholder analysis, definition of, 115
Standard for Portfolio Management, The, 41
Standard for Program Management, The, 55, 65
Strategic alignment
  in OPM implementation, 16
  in program governance, 59

SWOT analysis, definition of, 115
System, definition of, 115

Threat, definition of, 115
Transition to operations, 38

Uncertainty, definition of, 115